Praise for
Happy Hour is 9 to 5

~~~~~~~~~~

"This book will be at my desk, completely highlighted, so I can re-member to create the happy workplace we all need."
 — *Phil Gerbyshak, author of Make it Great*

"Only you are responsible for your happiness, so it's up to you to read Alexander Kjerulf's "Happy Hour is 9 to 5" and find out what steps you can take to make yourself, your colleagues, and your staff happier at work. The book's knowledge, tips, and real-life case studies will equip and inspire you to change your working life for the better."
 — *Angela Beesley, co-founder of Wikia*

"This book is an excellent addition to a management library. The con-cepts and suggestions are persuasive and logical, and should be taken to heart by anyone looking to make their workplace a better place to work."
 — *Mary Beth Sancomb-Moran, Impromptu Librarian*

"By far one of the most refreshing books on work culture that I've ever seen."
 — *Sheldon Cooke, customer service professional, California*

"I did not feel like putting it down and wanted to read it one shot."
 — *Nirmala Palaniappan, Knowledge Management Consultant, India*

Our Trees

By buying this book you also bought the
right to get a tree planted.

Go to **www.pinetribe.com/planting**
to claim your tree.

ALEXANDER KJERULF

HAPPY HOUR IS 9 TO 5

HOW TO LOVE YOUR JOB, LOVE YOUR LIFE, AND KICK BUTT AT WORK

PINETRIBE

Happy Hour is 9 to 5
How to Love your Job, Love your Life, and Kick Butt at Work
© Alexander Kjerulf and Pine Tribe Ltd. 2014

Illustrations: Palle Schmidt
Cover design and typeset: Klahr | Graphic Design
Photographer: Lars Schmidt
Editors: Julia Hilliard and Kalimaya Krabbe

1st edition 2014

ISBN: 978-0-9912609-1-1

www.pinetribe.com/alexander

Pine Tribe Ltd.
International House
1 St Katharine's Way
London, E1W 1UN

To my mother Alexandra
with my love.

Acknowledgements

~~~~~~~~

During the writing of this book, I was very grateful for:
My wonderful wife Patricia, for making me happy every single day!

My playmates in Copenhagen and all over the world for their enthusiasm, support and generosity: Arlette Bentzen, Steve Shapiro, Traci Fenton, Roosevelt Finlayson, Rowan Manahan, Thomas Mygdal, Carsten Ohm, Will McInnes, Tom Nixon, Max St. John, Kareem Mayan, Bernie deKoven, Mike Wagner, and more people than I can mention here. I am proud and happy to belong to a global tribe of such cool, committed individuals.

My ex-colleagues at Enterprise Systems, for their commitment to creating a great company together, their willingness to explore new paths to do so and the enthusiasm that came out of it. Oh, and the foosball games of course.

This book was written entirely in various cafés in Copenhagen, especially Laundromat Café, and Bodega. Thanks for the caffeine and the Wi-Fi :o)

And finally, the readers of my blog. Without you guys, this book probably wouldn't exist, and it certainly wouldn't be half as good. Your generosity, feedback, ideas and stories are a never-ending source of energy and inspiration. Thank you!

Contents

~~~~~~~~~

Foreword

By Lars Kolind

~~~~~~~~~~~

When I first saw Alexander's title on his business card – Chief Happiness Officer – I must confess I didn't take it seriously. Whatever next?!

But later I realised that Alexander has a point: happy employees, managers, customers and suppliers make the best team. They get more work done, they come up with more new ideas, and they create more value.

Happiness can be part of a company's competitive edge. It shapes corporate culture, helps attract the most talented people, and it makes them stay longer.

I have spent quite a few years researching and experimenting in order to find a new formula for running a business in the 21st century. My goal is to find a substitute for yesterday's rigid, hierarchical, financially-driven business and organisational models. I arrived at four key elements:

1. A meaning that comes before profit.
2. A partnership between the company and its employees.
3. A collaborative organisation.
4. Value-based leadership.

Reading this book, it struck me that happiness across the board promotes all four of these elements. Companies are seldom happy if they are only about money. It is much more fun to work for a worthy cause.

If companies and employees are opposites or enemies instead of partners, nobody will be happy. If there are barriers between employees that prevent collaboration, energy will be wasted on internal friction rather than spent on customer satisfaction. An open and collaborative organisation has fun.

It is that simple.

Therefore I dare say that happiness is not a joke in management. It is damn serious: happy companies will win. Happy companies will grow and happy companies will innovate.

The company of the future is – happy.

Lars Kolind

Lars Kolind is the internationally renowned CEO responsible for the dramatic turnaround of troubled hearing aid manufacturer Oticon. Lars led Oticon from near collapse to world leadership during his ten years as CEO from 1988 to 1998. The story of his turnaround – which included introducing the spaghetti organisation, mobile workplaces and the paperless office – is required reading at most business schools.

Lars is the author of The Second Cycle – Winning the War Against Bureaucracy.

Just Imagine ...

~~~~~~~~~~

Happy at work.
Happy? At work?
Happy ... at work?

I want you to imagine waking up early on a Monday morning. Picture yourself as you turn off the alarm clock, and lie in bed for a moment before getting up. Your bed is comfortable and warm and you really want to enjoy that feeling just a little bit longer, but just thinking about the working week ahead of you is making you smile and get ready to jump out of bed.

You just know it's going to be a wonderful week. You will get to do great work you can be proud of. You will get to make a difference, as you did last week and every week before that.

You look forward to having fun with your co-workers. You will help them whenever you can, and they will help you whenever you need it. You know you will be spending the day with people you like and can talk to. People who appreciate you for who you are and what you do.

You look forward to working with your boss, a person you truly admire for her skills, her amiability, and the way she brings out the best in others.

You can't wait to interact with your customers and clients. You've been told so many times now that your competence and your attitude of fun are an inspiration to them – many of them continue to return because of you.

And more than anything else, you look forward to making a positive difference. You know that being the person you are and with the skills that you have, you will do work that you can be proud of.

You also can't wait to come home in the evening, all fired up. Though you spend your workdays focused and concentrated, you have so much fun doing your job that it actually leaves you with more energy than when the day started. You look forward to sharing that energy and positivity with your friends and family after another great workday.

Imagine for a moment how it would feel to lie in bed on a Monday morning going "YES! I get to go to work this week!"

Is it possible to be this happy at work? Can we go to work and be energised, have fun, do great work, enjoy the people we work with, wow our customers, be proud of what we do, and look forward to our Monday mornings as much as some people long for Friday afternoon? Can we create workplaces where this level of happiness is the norm, not the exception?

Or must we simply accept that work is unpleasant and tough and that is why we get paid to do it?

This book is here to tell you that yes, you can be that happy at work, and when you are, it's great for you and great for your job, your company and your career, because you get:

- More drive and motivation.
- Better relationships with co-workers.
- Greater success.
- More creativity and good ideas.
- More energy.
- Better health.
- Less stress.
- Much more fun.

Your life outside of work gets better too because work becomes a source of energy and good experiences rather than a stressful, painful, frustrating obligation.

And it's not just good for people. More and more businesses are finding that things work better with happiness and that happy companies have:

- Higher productivity – happy people achieve better results.
- Higher quality – because happy employees care about quality.
- Lower absenteeism – people actually want to go to work.
- Less stress and burnout – happy people are less prone to stress.
- The best people – people want to work for happy companies.
- Higher sales – happy people are the best salespeople.
- Higher customer satisfaction – happy employees are the best basis for good service.
- More creativity and innovation – happy people are more creative.
- More adaptability – happy people are much more adaptable and open to change.
- Better stock performance and higher profits – for all of the above reasons.

Simply put: happy companies are more efficient and make more money. And they make people happy, which is of course a goal in itself.

The flip side

Most of us have probably been on the flip side, and have been unhappy at work. I once spent a long year being unhappy at work, and I hated every second of it.

After graduating with a Masters in computer science in 1994, I worked as a developer and consultant, and then co-founded a software company called Enterprise Systems with some fellow geeks in 1997.

When we started the company we had one huge advantage: we had no idea how to run a business. The three founders – myself, Patrik

Helenius and Martin Broch Pedersen – were all happy geeks with great tech skills and almost no business experience. We did have some pretty good notions of how NOT to do it from our previous jobs, but mostly we had a passion for doing things RIGHT and for creating a workplace that people would actually like. This protected us from repeating "business as usual", and freed us to try many untraditional approaches.

It worked. In our company:

- People did excellent work.
- All employees took responsibility and action when needed.
- We made good money. Not obscene, just good.
- We focused on constant education and training.
- Everyone was involved in leading the company.
- Everyone was motivated and engaged.
- People didn't work too much – 40 hours a week or less.
- We had massive amounts of fun.

But nice as it was, after about three years I began to feel constrained and locked in. I wanted to do something new, and there was no room to do this within our company. I thought long and hard about leaving the company, but didn't get around to actually quitting. That was a mistake.

During my last year at the company, I was desperately unhappy. Most mornings when I woke up I looked for some reason to stay home. At work I got very little done, and spent most of my time counting the hours until I could leave.

And here's the worst part: I could barely recognise myself. I'm normally energetic, positive and fun. I became tired, negative and bitter, not only at work but also outside of it. I was depressed and annoyed at everyone and everything.

Normally I'm a very creative person who comes up with ten new ideas a day, but during that period my creativity dried up. I couldn't come up with a good idea to save my life, and every idea other people presented to me sounded horrible. I was in a perpetually negative state.

Finally, in June 2002, I quit. I decided not to look for a new job straight away and to just take some time to decompress. Those summer months with uncharacteristically great weather (for Denmark) slowly brought me back to my old self. I spent zero time thinking about my next job, reading job postings or starting a new company.

Then one lovely summer day at the beach, the idea came to me: happiness at work. That's it! That's what I'm passionate about. That's what I want to work with. This idea became Woohoo inc., and we have been making people happy at work since early 2003. We have worked with clients like IBM, LEGO, IKEA, Hilton, Microsoft, Pfizer and many others, who are now happier at work after trying our methods.

We have taken the message of happiness at work to over 30 countries on 5 continents and our work has been mentioned by CNN, the New York Times, Fortune Magazine, Forbes, the Times of India and countless others.

I can safely say that there is no greater job than making other people happy! It's continually fun, exciting and rewarding. And when you think about it, isn't that really the true purpose of most jobs – to make people happy? You must make the customers happy. Or your co-workers. Or the boss. Or the shareholders.

Now I want to make it clear that we don't go to work to be happy. We go to work to work, so to speak. You are at work to do the best possible job you can and to constantly excel and improve your performance. But we happen to do that much better when we are happy at work.

A nurse who makes the patients happy and healthy is better than one who only makes them healthy. A boss who makes her employees happy and efficient is better than one who only touts efficiency. A teacher who can make his students smarter and happier is better than one who only passes on knowledge.

Choose this approach to work and business: make people happy – as many people as possible as often as possible, inside and outside your company – and you can't fail. And you will have a great time doing it!

The future is happy

I have great news for you: happiness at work is coming to almost all workplaces. It is inevitable. There is a massive tendency in the business world to focus more and more on making work a positive experience, and while it is not yet felt in every country or in every workplace, it soon will be.

The reason is simple but powerful: today, customer service, efficiency and innovation are an organisation's prime success factors. It doesn't matter how efficient a company is at producing yesterday's goods if it doesn't have the creativity to invent tomorrow's. Nobody cares how efficient its business processes are if it can't give its customers a good experience.

Studies consistently show that happy companies are way more productive, creative and service-oriented than unhappy ones. Therefore, the happy companies will beat the pants off the unhappy ones in the market place. The future of business is happy! It's inevitable.

However, if we choose to do something constructive about it now, we can become happy at work sooner rather than later. Our workplaces can reap the human and financial benefits this year rather than in five or ten years.

That is the thought that gets me out of bed, happy and smiling, almost every single Monday morning!

About This Book

~~~~~~~~~~

This book is for anyone who has a job and anyone who wants one. Whether you're an employee, manager or executive, this book has tips for you. Whether you work in industry, service, government or retail, there are tools you can use. Whether you're a graduate looking for your first job or have a long, distinguished career already behind you, there is always more to learn about happiness at work.

The book aims to convince you that:

- Each and every one of us can be happy at work.
- Being happy at work will not only make work more fun, it will also improve your quality of life outside work and make you more successful.
- Happy businesses are much more efficient than unhappy ones – happiness makes great business sense.
- Happiness at work is not rocket science – it is simple to help yourself and your workplace to be happy.

Of course, it's not enough just to know these things, we must also do something about it, so this book will leave you with everything you need to help make yourself and others happy at work:

1. Knowledge – The basic theory of happiness at work, based on scientific studies from psychology, sociology, neurology and management science.
2. Tools – Simple, practical tips and tools that will help you achieve fast results.
3. Energy – I will try to make you excited about the concept of happiness at work and all fired up to do something about it.
4. A plan – A specific plan tailored to your situation.

Stories and case studies

This book refers to many real-life case studies of companies who have achieved success through happiness. Business books normally preface every business case with a list of that company's accomplishments, which might go something like this:

> Acme Inc. is the only company in the world to have achieved triple-digit growth 58 years running.
>
> Their stock price has risen from 10 cents to $452 and is still a "strong buy" recommendation from all investment advisors.
>
> They have expanded from humble beginnings in the founder's outhouse in 1938, to a complex taking up half the buildings in lower Manhattan.
>
> The founder is now richer than Bill Gates and 3 out of 4 employees retire as millionaires on their stock options before they turn 40.

Or words to that effect.

Not only do these litanies of amazing accomplishments get boring after a while, but they also paint a false picture. The company may be successful, but who really knows why? The reason for their success could be innovation, timing, happiness, wise investments, or sheer, blind luck. Who knows?

When I use a company as a case study in this book, we can safely assume:

1. They are doing phenomenally well (You can always Google them if you don't believe me).
2. They themselves believe that one of the main reasons they are doing so well is happiness at work.

OK? OK!

All the stories you'll read in this book are true. Names and other details may have been changed to protect the innocent, but all events took place as described.

Go visit the website

This book has an accompanying website at this address:
www.pinetribe.com/alexander

Here you will find:

- Additional reading and articles on my blog, where I write about happiness at work regularly.
- Worksheets for the exercises.
- And lots more.

And most importantly, you can tell me and the rest of the world what you think about the book, and exchange thoughts about your experiences with other readers.

1

What Is Happiness At Work?

~~~~~~~~~~

All over the world, people are taking charge and changing their work lives for the better. A group of young nurses rebel against the hospital's sour mood and turn their ward into a happy place. A sales manager finally has enough of the bickering and competition in his workplace and quits for a much better job. A temp worker cheers up her co-workers with small, random acts of workplace kindness. A programmer at a bank learns what it takes to turn his department from boring to fun. You'll find their stories and many more throughout the book.

But what exactly is happiness at work? Let's start by learning a very strange looking word.

Arbejdsglæde

We Scandinavians have an advantage over the rest of the world when it comes to happiness at work: while most other nations are fairly new to the concept of happiness at work, we already have a word for it. In Danish, my native language, the word is *arbejdsglæde*, and while that may look utterly indecipherable to the rest of the world, it's a concept that is deeply ingrained in Scandinavian working culture and one that most Nordic businesses focus on to a large degree.

Consequently, Scandinavian workers are the happiest in the world. According to a study from 2005, 68% are happy or very happy with their current job, compared with 47% in the UK or even 35% in Belgium[1]. This is a major factor behind the success of Nordic companies like IKEA, Carlsberg, LEGO, and many others.

Arbejde means work and *glæde* means happiness, so *arbejdsglæde* literally translates into work-happiness. In case you're wondering, it's pronounced ah-bites-gleh-the. And you thought *Fahrvergnügen* was a mouthful!

The wonderful thing is that this idea is spreading all over the world. Happy companies exist in every industry and in every country, and while happiness is not yet the main focus of most businesses, more and more companies have decided to go happy.

So what is it?

What exactly is happiness at work? This question seems like a good place to start, and I've been working long and hard to come up with a definition of happiness at work, precisely because so many people ask me just that.

Working with clients, big and small, private and public, got me closer and closer to the answer, and after long deliberation I came up with what I believe is a concise, spot-on definition.
This will amaze you. Are you ready? Here it is:

Happiness at work is …
A feeling of happiness derived from work.

Boggles the mind, doesn't it?!

Happiness at work is that feeling you get when you:

- Really enjoy what you do.
- Do great work you can feel proud of.
- Work with amazing people.
- Know that what you do is important.
- Are appreciated for your work.
- Get to take responsibility.
- Have fun at work.
- Learn and grow.
- Make a difference. Are motivated and energised.
- Know that you kick butt.

Most of us already know that feeling. We've been there at least some of the time in our working lives. The question is: How do we get there more of the time?

Simply put, it's about experiencing positive emotions at work, rather than negative emotions. It's about feeling good, rather than feeling bad.
From Barbara Fredrickson's book Positvity, here's a list of the 10 most common positive emotions according to researchers:

- Love
- Serenity
- Forgiveness
- Awe
- Joy
- Interest
- Hope
- Pride
- Amusement
- Inspiration

How often do you experience these feelings at work?

Here's a list of the 10 most common negative emotions:

- Alarm
- Aversion
- Indifference
- Fear
- Anger
- Sorrow
- Frustration
- Hate
- Embarrassment
- Avarice

How often does that describe how you feel at work?

Happiness at work does not mean feeling deliriously joyful all the time. It's not about being relentlessly positive and optimistic even when the situation doesn't call for it. It's simply about doing what it takes to feel good and make others feel good as much as possible, and to avoid doing things that make you and others feel bad as far as possible. And the effects are unmistakable: being happy or unhappy at work has a huge impact on our lives. People who are happy at work not only enjoy work more, they have a much higher quality of life overall. They also do much better at work. People who are unhappy at work not only suffer mentally, but are also more prone to stress, depression, and a variety of diseases including heart disease and cancer. Make no mistake about it: in the worst cases, bad jobs kill people. You'll get the chance to find out what more happiness at work can do for your life, both at work and outside of it, in Chapter 6.

But let's lay down some theory first. Here are the most important things you should know about happiness at work.

One person's happiness is another's living hell

Here are Allan and Tom. They're both men in their 30s and work for the same advertising agency. They have similar backgrounds, but what makes them happy at work is wildly different:

- Allan enjoys working closely with others, Tom prefers working alone.
- Allan hates writing reports, while Tom loves it.
- Allan likes lots of new challenges, and Tom prefers predictability.
- Allan likes risk, but Tom tries to avoid it.
- Allan hates having to focus on only one project, but Tom loves it.

While there are definitely some things that make most people happy at work, we need to remember that happiness at work is different for everyone. One person's happiness at work is another's living hell. That's why happiness at work means treating everybody differently, because treating everyone the same only makes very few people happy.

Happiness at work is contagious

Three Italian scientists placed electrodes in the brains of macaque monkeys to study the neurons that control the actions of their hands,

24

for example, when they pick up an item. During each experiment, they recorded the activities of a single neuron in the monkey's brain while the monkey was allowed to reach for pieces of food, so the researchers could measure the neuron's response to certain movements.

One scientist explains: "I think it was Fogassi, standing next to a bowl of fruit and reaching for a banana, when some of the monkey's neurons reacted. How could this happen, when the monkey did not move? At first we thought it was a flaw in our measuring or an equipment failure, but everything checked out OK and the reactions were repeated as we repeated the movement."

A mirror neuron is a brain cell which is active both when an animal performs an action and when the animal observes the same action performed by another animal. Thus, the neuron "mirrors" the behaviour of another animal, as though the observer himself were performing the action. These neurons have been observed in primates, in some birds, and, yes, in humans, and some scientists consider them to be one of the most important findings of neuroscience in the last decade[2].

This may explain why happiness at work is so contagious – why one determinedly happy employee can lift the spirits of an entire department, and one happy executive can spread a positive mood throughout the whole organisation. To parts of our brain, there is no difference between being happy ourselves and seeing someone else being happy.

The bad news is that unhappiness is even more contagious than happiness, probably because humans are conditioned by evolutionary forces to be more attuned to negative emotions[3]. This makes fear and anger in the workplace more contagious than happiness, meaning that we must actively work to spread happiness instead.

This also means that your work-happiness depends on the people around you. I'm sure it's theoretically possible to be the only happy employee in a department with 20 unhappy people, but I'm also sure that it's really, really difficult! But being happy, surrounded by 20 happy people – now that could be a lot of fun …

Happiness at work is long term

Having fun and being happy is not about blowing off work that must be done. It's not about avoiding unpleasant tasks to enjoy yourself in the moment. And it's not just about being happy here and now.

It's about happiness for today and tomorrow and next year and 10 years from now. It's about realising that without long term happiness and enjoyment at work, you will not be your best, contribute as much, make as many people smile, or make as much of a difference.

You can't force people to be happy

"I have a co-worker who takes it upon herself to act as the happiness police, and it has had the result of creating an antagonistic attitude towards positive thinking! I had to calm down one team member who was genuinely insulted by her attempts, because by constantly goading him to be happier she was strongly implying that his current life just wasn't happy enough (and thus, the implication was, not worthwhile). Having someone try to control your "happiness" can be a very unpleasant experience indeed!"

Share your comment on www.pinetribe.com/alexander/discussion

If you intentionally or inadvertently create a mood at work where it's somehow right to be happy and wrong not to be, people will be less happy. You can even end up making happiness at work a dirty word – something people ridicule and actively resist.

That's why happiness at work must always be an invitation. You can open the door and invite people in, but you can't push them through the door against their will. The more you try, the more they will cling to the doorjamb, kicking and screaming.

Job satisfaction is not happiness

People always ask me why I use the term "Happiness At Work" rather than more traditional terms like "job satisfaction" or "employee satisfaction". And by always, I mean two or three times a year. At least!

And while the two terms are definitely related, they're still very different. Job satisfaction is what you *think* about your job – when you sit down and weigh all the pros and cons, how satisfied are you with your work situation. This is very much a rational, intellectual, thought-based process and it takes place only when you make a conscious effort to think about these things, e.g. once a year when you complete a staff satisfaction survey.

As we saw previously, happiness at work is how you *feel* about your job. On a regular, perfectly normal workday, how do you feel? This is automatic and takes place all the time, and hence tends to affect us much more deeply than satisfaction, which only matters when we are consciously making an effort to think about it.

In other words, satisfaction is how happy you are about your job while you think about how happy you are (which is rarely). Happiness at work is how happy you are the rest of the time while you're actually doing your job, which is hopefully the vast majority of the time.

That makes happiness much more relevant than satisfaction. Also, there is no way you can energise or excite yourself or other people in your workplace around the theme of satisfaction. "Come on, everybody, let's make this a workplace where we can all be satisfied with our jobs!" It's not exactly the rallying cry of the century.

Seriously: do you want to spend your working life simply being satisfied? When you look back on 50 years spent in business, do you want to be able to say, "Well, I was perfectly satisfied"?

No! Make happiness your goal. As in, "Let's make this a workplace where people are happy to work." As in, "I've been working for 50 years now, and it absolutely rocks! To me work is challenging, stimulating and just plain fun." It has way more potential and sends a much clearer and more interesting message:

Happiness at work = Exciting. Ambitious. Energising. Fun.
Job satisfaction = Booooooooring!

Happiness at work is something we do

Happiness at work does not come from mission statements, corporate values, white books, committees or workplace policies. It comes from the things you and I do, here and now.

It's not something we can do tomorrow or next week or next fiscal quarter. Happiness is something you have now – or never.

Happiness at work is not eternal

You can't be happy at work every day. No matter how much you love your job, there are still going to be bad days. And that's cool – it's always OK to have a bad day at work.

But, if the bad days start to mount up, or even outnumber the good, then it's time to consider what that does to you – and what you can do about it.

It's 50% about the job and 50% about you

The perfect job does not exist. There is no workplace out there that only has the things you like. There will always be a few boring tasks, a few co-workers you don't like, a few rude customers, a few unpleasant managers.

If your plan is to be happy at work as soon as your work and your workplace are perfect and trouble-free, you will never get there. And if you did you'd probably be bored out of your skull.

Happiness at work is not about eliminating all the bad stuff from your job. It's about being happy at work even though some of those bad things are present. It's about building up your skills and your energy to fix the problems, and to create more and more positive experiences at work.

Happiness at work looks different on different people

One of the very first Happiness at Work Workshops I did was for the Scandinavian logistics department of a large American car manufacturer. At the end of the workshop I asked the participants to share their thoughts, and one gentleman in his 50s stood up to speak. He was formally dressed in a suit and tie (the only one in the group) and with his grey hair and glasses he looked every bit the accountant. Which in fact he was.

He'd been very quiet throughout the workshop, but now he stood up to address the group. He paused for a moment, "I want all of you to know," he said in a sombre voice "that I'm not as unhappy as I look." The room erupted in laughter.

The serious face, the sombre voice, the quiet demeanour and the formal manner – that's how this man looked when he was happy at work.

Happiness at work does not necessarily mean running around ecstatically all day long. You can sit at your desk, quietly doing your work, and be discreetly happy. You can be sitting in a hectic meeting, arguing forcefully for your point of view, and be happy.

However, it pays to express your happiness at work, because:

1. The more your happiness shows, the more you spread it to others.
2. The more you express your happiness, the stronger it becomes inside you. If you hold your happiness in and never express it, it gradually dissipates. Express it clearly and visibly and it gets stronger and lasts longer.

While some people believe that you must be serious at work – in your speech, your clothes, and your demeanour – I disagree completely. There is no reason that you can't be highly professional and really good at your job and at the same time show that you're happy and energised.

Happiness at work is possible in almost every job

Some people think that it's only possible to be happy in certain kinds of jobs – those fun, creative ones. This is simply not true. You see many unhappy people in supposedly fun professions, and many happy people with supposedly unpleasant jobs, like sewage workers or funeral directors.

So happiness can be found in most jobs. The one exception to this rule is working in companies that are unethical or make products that are bad for people or the environment. If your work actively contributes to making the world worse, that will make you unhappy. Let's say your workplace makes land mines. Will that make you happy? I hope not!

Anyone can be happy at work

That's right, anyone! Happiness at work is not only for people with fun, creative jobs. It's not the prerogative of managers and executives. It's not limited to the highly paid and the powerful.

Any person who chooses to be happy at work and then does something about it can go from, "Oh crap, it's Monday, I have another week at work ahead of me," to "Yes! It's Monday! I have another week at work ahead of me!"

Happiness at work starts with a choice

"Happiness, like unhappiness, is a proactive choice."
  – Stephen Covey

Do you know someone who seems to have given up on happiness at work? Someone who has accepted that work is bad, that this won't change, and who has now chosen simply to survive rather than try to improve their situation?

The path to happiness at work starts with a simple decision: you must want to be happy. If you don't commit to being happy at work, you won't be. You won't make the choices that make you happy. You won't take the actions needed to get there. You won't change the things that need to change.

On the other hand, if you say, "Yes, I choose to be happy at work and to do what it takes to get there." then things will start to happen. Just making that decision won't magically make you happy – but it must be the starting point.

And something interesting happens when you decide on happiness: you take charge. When you decide to become happy at work and to do the things necessary to get there, you've put yourself in charge of your career and your work situation. You're no longer dependent upon the whims of your manager, co-workers or workplace.

You don't need to make this decision right now. Read this book and then think about how your life would be different if you were happy at work … Let's start with a look at what it takes to become happy at work.

2

What Makes Us Happy At Work?

~~~~~~~~~

On paper, Maria's new job had it all: a financially successful organisation, interesting tasks, an impressive salary, cool offices, a French chef, a gym, free fruit, massages, and a view out of her office window that took your breath away.

Maria is an easy-going, attractive woman in her forties with a broad business background, but even in her first month at the new job she noticed that things were very wrong. As wealthy as the organisation was, it still completely lacked human and social values. The workplace was plagued by distrust, infighting, slander, backstabbing, sexual harassment, a lack of respect, repression, and veiled threats.

She spent the second month in her new job pondering how she could change things. By the third month Maria realised that she probably wouldn't be able to change much and that she might easily get crushed trying. She quit without having found a new job.

Maria is now a publishing editor and is also responsible for HR and the work environment at her new workplace. Her salary is much lower, but her quality of life is much, much higher, and she told me: "I'm now a believer when it comes to happiness at work, and want to help spread the happy message."

While all the traditional trappings of a good job don't hurt, they're just not enough. As Maria's story shows, it doesn't matter how nice your office is, how large your salary is or how good the food is if the mood at the company is bad.

Some of the things we strive for at work – the title, the salary, the perks – aren't really the things that make us happy. I'm not saying that a high salary will make you unhappy (at least, that never happened to me!) but it won't necessarily make you happy either.

Many people think that it's the job itself that matters most; that as long as they can get their dream job, they'll be fine. "If I can just find work as a doctor/teacher/builder/photographer/etc., I'm sure I will be happy" they seem to say. But often they're wrong, because it's really not about the job very much. The perfect job does not exist.

Chris is a travel journalist who gets to travel to all the best resorts and travel destinations in the world, and try out the best restaurants and hotels. You have to admit, that sounds like really nice work, and when I met him, my first thought was naturally, "How can I kill this guy and get his job!" But the truth was, Chris wasn't that excited about it, because he never really got to enjoy his travels. He had to eat dinner in 4 or 5 different restaurants in one night. He had to visit 3 or 4 different hotels a day and could never relax in any of them. He also had to travel a lot and the endless plane rides soon became a boring chore to him.

On the other hand, I once talked to Peter, a sanitation worker (a few years ago he would have been called a trash man or bin man) who absolutely loves his job. Peter has to get up at 4 in the morning, but that also means that he is finished by noon and has the rest of the day off. He enjoys working outdoors, he has a great time with his co-workers on the garbage truck, and he likes doing a great job and helping people out.

Work itself can make us happy. If you're a salesperson who loves talking to customers, a mechanic who loves fixing things, a programmer who loves to code, or a nurse who loves treating patients, there's a good chance you'll be happy just doing the work involved in your job.

However, one thing should be made very clear: happiness at work is not limited to those people lucky enough to have found their calling. It's not only for those whose job is their first career choice. Even when the job itself is fairly generic, it's possible to love it.

Even if the work itself is perfect, that is absolutely no guarantee you'll be happy at work. If your manager is a terrible person, if the mood at the company is bad, if you're being bullied or treated unfairly, you will be unhappy at work, no matter how great the job.

It ain't what you've got, it's what you do with it

When you ask people what makes them happy at work apart from work itself, you get these long lists of what people want to have, usually including a good boss, appreciation, a good salary, nice co-workers, free donuts, having fun, great meetings, having ideas, and much, much more.

This is reflected in most theories and studies on job satisfaction and motivation, which invariably focus on what we must *have* to enjoy our jobs.

However, happiness at work is less about what you *have*, and more about what you *do*. You may *have* a great boss, a great team, interesting tasks and a lot of fun. But it's what *you've done* that makes it so. And it's what you *do today* that will keep it that way.

Also, even if you know what you must have to be happy at work, you still face the obvious question: "So, what do I *do* to get it?"

Finally, focusing on what you must have is passive, whereas focusing on what you must do is active. You take charge and create the future you want.

That is why any useful theory of what makes us happy at work must focus on what we do – not on what we have. By some strange coincidence, the theory presented in this chapter does just that!

So if it's not the job... what is it?

So what can make us happy? Well, it turns out it's really simple. It only takes two things to make us happy at work:

1. Results
2. Relationships

That's it! That's all there is. When we have those two things we're happy at work. When we only have one, we're more or less OK. When we have neither, we feel terrible at work.

Let's take a closer look at these two. First, results.

Results make us happy at work

"Happiness lies in the joy of achievement and the thrill of creative effort."
– Franklin D. Roosevelt

35

We all want to get results. We all want to:

- Make a difference
- Contribute value
- Know that our work is important
- Get appreciation
- Feel needed
- Do work that we can be proud of

One of our deepest psychological needs is the need to control our environment. If we're placed in a situation where we have no control, where nothing we do matters, we feel terrible.

On the other hand, we love to do great work and to make a difference. Accomplishment *feels great*.

Some managers don't realise this about people. They think that people need to be motivated into performing. That when we're left alone, we choose to do nothing. In fact, the reverse is true and when given half a chance, we work our hearts out to accomplish results.

There are four things we can do to get great results at work:

1. Praise – appreciation shows us we get results
2. Grow and learn – this is about getting results for yourself
3. Find meaning – so you can see you don't just get results for the business, you're contributing to something greater
4. Be free – so you're free to get great results

People who do these four things get great results. We'll look at each of these later.

Relationships make us happy at work

According to Maslow's widely-known hierarchy of needs, our most fundamental needs are physiological needs – food, sleep, and so on – and our need for safety. This is followed by our need to belong and to feel loved. Our species has evolved in groups and communities, and few of us can be happy unless we belong to a functioning group.

Which brings us to relationships at work. When you ask people what makes them happy at work, they consistently rate these things the highest:

- Nice co-workers
- A good manager
- Good communication
- A sense of humour in the workplace

Each of these is a sign of good relationships, caring and, indeed, love – simple signs that people like each other and communicate well. These good relationships don't have to stop at co-workers and managers, but can also happen with customers, suppliers, shareholders, and the company's wider community.

Relationships at work matter so much because we will be spending *a lot* of time with people at work. When you think about it, you'll be spending more of your waking hours with them than with your friends and family *combined*.

There are three things you can do to create great relationships at work:

1. Be positive
2. Be yourself
3. Love

We'll look at each of these later.

What is your focus? Results or relationships?

Of these two, which do you focus on the most? Are you mostly focused on getting results or creating relationships at work? What about your workplace as a whole? Does it mostly emphasise and strive for results or relationships?

Think about it for a second.

It's probably safe to say that 99.9% of all workplaces, managers and employees focus on results the most. This is hardly surprising – organisations exist for the results they get. They're all about the budgets, plans, projects, strategies and missions – i.e. the results.

So it's perfectly understandable that they should focus so strongly on results. It's also a mistake.

What happens in most workplaces is that they focus so much on results that they forget about relationships at work. But good relationships don't just appear by themselves, it takes a concerted, daily effort to create them. When this effort is not made, you get bad relationships at work. Instead of teamwork and mutual appreciation you get mistrust, internal conflict, bickering and selfishness.

This of course makes people unhappy at work and when people are unhappy at work, results suffer. Which of course makes the workplace focus *even more* on results.

So, ironically, focusing too much on results *harms results!*
And that is why workplaces must focus equally on results and relationships in everything they do. Fortunately, this is actually fairly easy!

Results *and* relationships

A focus on results and relationships can be introduced into almost any job and any workplace in the world. They're not limited to certain businesses or certain types of work or workers.

Notice that it's not the organisation that has to focus on results and relationships – it's you. It's us. While the company must offer an environment within which these are easy to attain, it's still up to us to actually take the opportunity to do something about it every day.

Do you prioritise the things that make you happy at work, or are your efforts concentrated elsewhere? The problem is that many people don't have a clear picture of what makes them happy at work, and while they may have the best of intentions, they end up doing the wrong things.

Let's take a closer look at each of the things it takes to give us great results and great relationships – and hence great happiness – at work.

Praise

Kjaer Group, a Danish company that sells cars in developing nations, introduced The Order of the Elephant a few years back. It's a huge plush toy that any employee can award to any other, along with an explanation of why that employee deserves The Order. The recipient keeps the elephant for a couple of days, and at two feet tall it's hard to overlook if it's standing on that person's desk.

Other employees stopping by immediately notice the elephant and go, "Hey, you got the elephant. What'd you do?" which of course means that good stories and best practice get told and re-told many times. This is an excellent, simple and cheap way of enhancing learning and happiness at work.

Praise may be the single most effective method to make people happy at work:

- Everyone can do it
- It's easy
- It works
- It takes no time and costs no money

Remember that good praise is:

- Relevant – Don't praise just for the sake of praise – make sure there's a reason to praise.
- Timely – Praise as soon as there's a reason.
- Personal – Tailor the praise to suit that particular person being praised.

For extra bonus points:

- Praise someone you don't talk to often. It's a great way to establish contact.
- Praise your manager. Managers often hear very little praise from their employees. However, only genuine praise counts – don't kiss butt!
- If you really want a challenge, praise someone you don't like much or someone you're currently having a conflict with. It can be a great way to get unstuck. Can't think of anything positive about that person? Try again – there's always something.

Also, try to remember that not only can you praise people for what they do, but you can also praise them for who they are. The happiest workplaces use this technique to create a culture of praise, where good deeds and good people are routinely and quickly noticed and appreciated.

Which philosophy do you think is more likely to make people happy at work?

Catch people making mistakes and punish them quickly

or

Catch people doing things right and praise them quickly

While I definitely opt for the latter, this does not mean that you can't criticise people and correct them when they make mistakes. In fact, if you routinely praise people when they get things right, they're more open and positive towards criticism.

Some great ways to praise people include:

In person – Don't make a big production out of it, just go up to a colleague, deliver your praise and then get back to work. Do not hang around waiting to be praised back. Also, do not add " …but you really need to improve your …" after the praise – that ruins the whole point.

Use a token – Like the elephant that the Kjaer Group uses, a widely recognised token helps to develop a culture of praise within your company. If you can find something with relevance to your company, even better.

On the walls – The London-based innovation agency ?What If! has praise for their employees written all over their combined meeting and reception area. Any employee can nominate any other for their good deeds, and the best ones are immortalised in big, colourful letters pasted across the walls and ceiling of the busiest area of the office, where the most people will see them.

Grow and learn

Michael, a programmer in his mid-thirties, came up to me after a presentation I gave and told me this story.

"I work as a programmer in a major bank. I used to go in every week, work my 40 hours (more like 50, but hey) and get paid a nice salary. It was a nice job in a good company, my boss was a good guy, my co-workers were nice people and the work was OK.

But as time passed, I felt like something was missing. Work was comfortable and secure, but I felt that there were sides of me that I never really got to use. I wanted to do work I could really feel proud of. I wanted to make more of a difference. And mostly, I was never really excited about work.

So I asked myself what it would take to improve things. I came up with three things:

1. Being more creative and working on more varied projects, as opposed to only maintaining the bank's internal programs.
2. More fun at work. The mood in the department was very serious and professional, to the point of being boring.
3. Learning some new professional skills.

I asked my boss about this and he was very supportive. We drew up a plan for some courses and certifications and found some new tasks that I could work on. We recruited some like-minded allies

41

in the group and worked on lightening the mood in the group together.

To my surprise, this didn't just change my working life a little, it made
a big difference. With my new skills, new projects and a more positive
mood at work, I went from feeling OK about my job to feeling really
great about it.

I do much better work as well. Partly because I've increased my
skills and increased my work experience but mainly because I feel
so much more enthusiastic about work now. The difference between
being OK with my job and being happy about it has been huge for
me."

No matter how much you enjoy your job today, if you do exactly the
same things in exactly the same way for a long time, sooner or later
you will stop enjoying it. Human beings are learning machines, learning from everything that goes on around us, and loving that feeling of
getting better and wiser.

We're either growing or we're shrinking; there's no in-between.
Shrinking feels bad; growing feels really, really good because it lets
you:

- Know that you're better at your job now than you've ever been.
- Be curious and learn about a topic.
- Know that you can obtain the skills you need to succeed.
- Expand your horizons.

Michael took the initiative and learned some new professional skills
that made him enjoy his work more. But he also learned what makes
him and his co-workers happy at work and was able to use this knowledge to create a fun and engaging mood in his department, together
with his manager.

When we don't learn at work, things become a lot less fun.

"When I worked for the federal government here in Canada I tried
suggesting that all the training allowances be used freely. Spend your

42

The Queen does not pay for knitting classes – that's classic! Well, perhaps if she did she wouldn't have lost a valuable employee.

Peter Senge is the man behind the concept of Learning Organisations, which he defines as:

"Organisations where people continually expand their capacity to create the results they truly desire, where new and expansive patterns of thinking are nurtured, where collective aspiration is set free, and where people are continually learning to see the whole together."

There are many ways to learn in the workplace. You can be learning professionally and getting better at your job, or you can be learning about yourself, the people around you, and the workplace.

Basically, learning can be injected into any activity at work, making it run more smoothly and be more fun to do. You can have a meeting and learn. You can work on a project and learn. You can work alone and learn. You can talk to co-workers and learn. Here are some great ways to keep learning at work.

Take a course in something – anything!

Pixar, the company known and loved for movies like Toy Story and Finding Nemo, has created something they call Pixar University, that lets employees take classes in moviemaking, sure, but also in pottery, improvisational theatre, sculpture, drawing and much more.

How does learning pottery make you a better Pixar employee? Randy S. Nelson, the dean of Pixar University, explains:

43

I have enjoyed courses in painting, creative writing, improv theatre and singing, and while none of this is directly relevant to the work I do, it all helps me to grow and develop. You never know when something that seems totally irrelevant is going to spark a creative breakthrough, precisely because it is not directly connected to your field of work.

Pixar realises that happy people make better movies and that learning is a key part of making them happy. It doesn't matter what they're learning, as long as they're learning, growing and developing – and having fun doing it.

Learn one new thing about a co-worker every day

What do you know about your co-workers? Do you know who has children and how many? Who has what hobby? Where did they go on their last holiday? What makes them happy or unhappy at work?

Take a genuine interest and absorb at least one new fact every day. The more you know about the people around you, the easier it gets to create a positive work environment, with better communication, better understanding, and fewer conflicts.

Teach

"When I was just starting in my new job, I had a lot of trouble using the IT systems. One day I asked one of my co-workers how to do a specific thing. She promptly put all of her own work aside and spent the whole afternoon teaching me to use the system.

This made me very happy, because it made me much better at my job, but especially because it told me that people at my new job were willing to take time to help each other and teach others what they know."

One of the best ways to learn is to teach. As the story above shows, it's also a great way to make others happy at work. What can you teach others? What tips and tricks can you pass on?

Swap jobs

At Southwest Airlines, employees regularly swap jobs. No, the baggage handlers don't get to fly the planes, but they may get to follow a pilot for a day, just to see what their job is like. And pilots get to be counter staff, executives try working as ground staff, and flight attendants get to be executives.

In one case a baggage handler explained how he'd always envied the pilots. He was down on the tarmac in the sun and hot weather loading and unloading luggage, and from where he was standing he could see the pilot sitting in the cool cockpit eating an ice cream. The lucky bastard! But after following a pilot at work, he gained a new understanding of the pilots' work. That pilot has probably been up since 4:30 in the morning, and has been flying almost non-stop since then. He's eating an ice cream because he doesn't have time for a real lunch – the plane is taking off again in ten minutes.

It also works the other way – if a plane is late, Southwest pilots often leave their cockpit to help the ground crew load or unload bags. That's the attitude of mutual respect and assistance a company develops when different groups of employees have some insight into each other's worlds.

Most conflicts between groups of employees arise when people don't understand each other. If you can spend some time in another person's shoes, it's a great way to meet and engage people, and to learn about their job, so you can work more efficiently together afterwards.

Try stuff out

"A ceramics teacher announced on the opening day of the course that he was dividing the class into two groups. All those on the left side of the studio, he said, would be graded solely on the quantity of work they produced, all those on the right solely on its quality.

His procedure was simple: on the final day of class he would bring in his bathroom scales and weigh the work of the "quantity" group: fifty pound of pots rated an "A", forty pounds a "B", and so on. Those being graded on "quality," however, needed to produce only one pot -albeit a perfect one – to get an "A".

Well, came grading time and a curious fact emerged: the works of highest quality were all produced by the group being graded for quantity. It seems that while the "quantity" group was busily churning out piles of work – and learning from their mistakes – the "quality" group had sat theorising about perfection, and in the end had little more to show for their efforts than grandiose theories and a pile of dead clay."
– From the book Art & Fear by David Bayles and Ted Orland

If you always do things the same way, how are you ever going to find a better way? Try new approaches out and see what happens. Yes, you will fail once in a while, but failing is a great way – sometimes the only way – to learn.

Make mistakes faster

Randy Nelson from Pixar has another great saying:

"You have to honor failure, because failure is just the negative space around success."

No matter how many times you tell yourself that "failure is not an option", failure always remains an option. Closing your eyes to this fact only makes you more likely to fail. Putting pressure on people to always succeed makes mistakes more likely because:

- People who work under pressure are less effective.
- People resist reporting bad news.
- People close their eyes to any signs of trouble.

This is especially true when people are punished for making mistakes. Management über-guru Peter Drucker provocatively suggested that businesses should find all the employees who never make mistakes and fire them, because employees who never make mistakes never do anything interesting. Admitting that mistakes happen and dealing constructively with them when they do makes mistakes less likely.

Failure is often the path to new, exciting opportunities that wouldn't have appeared otherwise. Closing your eyes to failure means closing your eyes to these opportunities. Menlo Innovations, an IT company in Ann Arbor, Michigan has a big sign hanging in their office that reads "Make mistakes faster!" They recognise that occasional mistakes are a part of doing anything interesting or innovative, and that the key lesson is to fail early and learn from it.

Be free

"Last year my company started looking for a new building for our headquarters. The old one was designed for 120 people – we were nearing 200, and things were getting seriously cramped." Anette, a 38-year-old secretary at a Danish shipping company looks a little stressed just thinking about the old overcrowded offices. Then she smiles. "And here's the cool thing: instead of making the decision on their own, management invited all employees who wanted to, to participate in looking for and choosing a new building.

"Ten people formed a workgroup and we ran the whole process from the very beginning, talking to other co-workers about what their dream office looked like, looking at different possibilities and then recommending one to management, who accepted our decision and signed off on it right away.

"Because the decision involved so many passionate people, we got a really good feel for what we were looking for in an office and that enabled us to choose just the right building. And best of all, when we made the decision almost everyone in the company accepted it instantly. They may not all have agreed that it was the best possible option, but they'd all had the chance to contribute and everyone who cared about the choice felt they'd been heard."

As I previously said, psychological studies show again and again that a fundamental basis for our happiness is the ability to control our own environment. When we are involved in the decisions that matter to us, when we can participate actively in creating our future, when we feel active rather than passive, we are much happier. Contrast this with a work environment where big decisions that directly affect you are made without your knowledge and without your input.

I admit that there is a problem here: while you can freely choose to be positive, to learn or to be open, it's difficult to participate unless you're invited to do so and your workplace and managers encourage it. This particular factor therefore relies more on your work environment than the others. But this is no excuse. If you only participate when you're actively invited to, you will miss many opportunities. Instead, you must sometimes invite yourself to participate. If there's something going on that you really, really want to be a part of – ask!

Of course, we can't all participate in everything, and we can't all be a part of every decision – nobody would get any work done. But in general, the more freedom and autonomy you experience at work, the happier you will be. Here are some ways to do it.

Plan your own work time

Patagonia makes outdoor clothing and gear. The company has grown from one man making mountain-climbing equipment part time to raise money to fund his own climbing adventures, to a $500 million business. If you visit Patagonia's headquarters in Southern California, very close to the beach, you may wonder why there are surfboards lined up in the hallways. Founder Yvon Chouinard explains:

> "I'm a businessman, but I'm still going to do things on my own terms. I'm going to break a lot of rules, and we're going to blur the distinction between work and play.
>
> So we have a policy here – it's called "Let My People Go Surfing." A policy which is, when the surf comes up, anybody can just go surfing. Any time of the day, you just take off and go surfing …
>
> That attitude changes your whole life. If your life is set up so that

you can drop anything when the surf comes up, it changes the whole way you run your life. And it has changed this whole company here."

If there's any way for you to plan your own work time, grab it. Being in control of our own work patterns is a crucial factor. And seriously, who is better able to plan your own work time than yourself?

Some jobs require your presence at certain times, but many others are much more flexible. If you can take this into account you can design your working week so that you get more out of your time both at work and outside of it.

It all depends on how you work best. Is eight hours a day optimal for you? Or do you prefer to work ten hours a day for four days a week and take Friday off?

Of course, this can only happen if the company you work for recognises that employees are adults capable of making these decisions on their own. At Motek, every employee has a designated back-up available to provide cover while they're out of the office. Employees can leave for the day or for a week whenever they want, as long as they first check with their backup to make sure he or she is around before they leave.

Semco lets each and every employee choose their own working hours. Some prefer to get in really early to avoid the hideous rush-hour traffic in São Paulo. Some are late risers and are more efficient if they get in shortly before lunch. Each employee gets to decide for themself. When this approach was introduced, some people were deeply worried. A factory line can only operate when all the people are present, so what would happen if some people decided to come in early and some late?

What happened was simple. The employees look at each other and went "Want to start at 6.30 tomorrow?" followed by "Yeah, 6:30 sounds good!" Problem solved.

Open to-do list

Motek, located in California, makes warehouse management software and have implemented openness in a very interesting way. They have an internal, company-wide to-do list of all ongoing projects, a list that all employees have access to. This open sharing of information means that Motek's employees can get the information they need in order to make better decisions, resulting in happier, more motivated people.

Motek's customers and suppliers also have access to the same to-do list, and customers and suppliers regularly offer to help with an item on the list. Any Motek employee can take on any item on the to-do list and set a deadline for it. If the employee completes the task inside the deadline, they receive $100 towards their next vacation. If they do not complete the task, but say so and ask for help to meet the deadline, they still get the $100. This is a great way of stimulating the right behaviour – it's OK not to meet your deadlines if you take responsibility and ask for help.

Open books

Ricardo Semler is my business idol. I've read his books and followed his work and I'm a fan. Completely and without reservation, probably in the same way that 14-year old girls are fans of Justin Bieber. If he ever comes to Copenhagen to give a speech, I'll be in the front row, screaming my little lungs out!

Ahem. Let me rephrase that...

I deeply admire Ricardo Semler. His vision of leadership has been the driving force behind an organisation so different, so innovative and so successful that the business world has been forced to sit up and pay attention.

When Ricardo Semler took over leadership of Semco, a small company of 100 employees based in São Paulo, Brazil, he was the quintessential tough, old-school manager. He worked long hours, chewed people out for the smallest mistakes, and focused only on profits.

Then one day, Ricardo collapsed from overwork and was told by doctors that he was heading straight for a heart attack – no mean feat for a 21-year-old. This became a turning point, and since then Ricardo has led Semco on an uncompromising quest to make it the best possible place to work. They now employ 3,000 people in a number of businesses, from internet development to facility management, and are happier than ever[5].

One thing Semco practises is openness. They want their employees to know as much as possible about the company, so they publish their financial statements for all employees to read, along with a guide to what the numbers mean. This offers employees deep insight into the company's present situation. They have also made board meetings public, so any employee who wants to can sit in and see how major decisions in the company are made.

The result? Employees make better, more responsible decisions because they know how those decisions affect the company's health, and they feel valued because they are "in the know".

Find meaning

A traveller walks down a dusty road. The sun is shining down mercilessly from a clear sky and the heat is almost unbearable. As he pauses for a sip of water, he notices three men sitting by the side of the road, chopping up stones. The first one clearly has the look of a man wishing he was anywhere else. No wonder – it's hot, hard, unpleasant labour after all. The traveller asks him, "What are you doing?" "Cutting stones," the man replies.

The second man looks fairly happy with what he's doing despite the hot weather and hard work. "What are you doing?" the traveller asks him. "I'm cutting stones to make money to support my family," the man replies.

The third stonecutter has a look that verges on blissful. He's giving the stones his full attention, precisely and powerfully cutting them into smaller rocks. When he stops for a moment, the traveller asks him, "What are you doing?" In a proud voice he replies, "I'm building a cathedral."

There are three levels of meaning you can find at work:

1. No meaning. Your work makes no sense to you.
2. Your work has meaning because it supports you and your family.
3. Your work has meaning in itself because you're contributing to something great or making the world a better place.

This is not to say that every job has meaning, or even that your job has meaning. Some jobs do, some jobs don't. What matters is that some people understand the meaning of their work, whereas others don't. It's much easier to be happy if your job has meaning to you, and you keep that meaning in mind. Knowing how your work contributes to the company's success, to your local community, or even to making a better world makes you proud of what you do.

Almost any job has meaning:

- You clean at a hospital? Without efficient cleaning, hospital patients are at risk of death from serious illnesses like MRSA.
- You're a teacher? You're shaping your country's next generation.
- You write software? You're helping your customers become more efficient.
- You're a secretary? You're making your co-workers more efficient and productive.

It's difficult to find meaning for some jobs. For example, if your company produces landmines, it may be difficult to find meaning in that. And that makes it harder to be happy at work.

The following are ways to discover or create meaning at work.

Where are you contributing?

We all want to make a difference, and we all love to get results. We all want to know that what we do at work has contributed somehow – that it has meaning.

To discover meaning in your job, if it's not already clear to you, ask yourself:

1. Who am I making happy in the company?
2. Who am I making happy outside the company through my work?
3. Who is the company making happy? How am I contributing to this?

George Bernard Shaw had the right idea when he said:

> "This is the true joy in life, the being used for a purpose recognised by yourself as a mighty one; the being thoroughly worn out before you are thrown on the scrap heap; the being a force of Nature instead of a feverish selfish little clod of ailments and grievances complaining that the world will not devote itself to making you happy."

Finding your purpose at work, one you recognise as mighty, is a great way to become happier at work. To paraphrase Shaw, "This is the true joy in work".

Make your results visible

Achieving results makes us proud and gives work meaning. Imagine going to work every day and never really having anything to show for it.

It's important to make results visible so that you can see what you've achieved. Here are some ways to do it:

- Keep a to-do list so that you can tick off completed tasks and see how much work you've done every day or every week.
- Print out a list of finished tasks and hang the list on the department bulletin board. The list showcases everyone's progress and accomplishments.
- Write results on a whiteboard for everyone to see.
- Publish statistics on the company intranet.
- Hang a bell in the office and ring it every time someone closes a case.

To any managers who still think that happy employees don't work hard – you've got it exactly backwards. Most people are happy only when they do good work and get great results.

In September 2006 I asked the readers of my blog what made them happy at work. The top scorer by far was getting results. Here are some of the things mentioned:

- Seeing something through to completion.
- Seeing positive change.
- Getting a complex problem to solve.
- Creating simple solutions to problems that were believed to be impossible/hard.
- Getting things done (finally).
- Fixing problems and helping people.
- Noticing how my proposals produce positive change once implemented.

Contribute outside the company

Great Harvest is a US bakery franchise whose goals are, "Be loose and have fun, Bake phenomenal bread, Run fast to help customers, Create strong, exciting bakeries, and Give generously to others." They tell the following story on their website:

"When the devastating tsunami struck Southeast Asia in December of 2004, Great Harvest Bread Co. owners Dee and Bernie O'Connor (Lansing, Michigan) decided they needed to do something to help. In less than one week, the O'Connors organized a benefit to aid the survivors of the tsunami, enlisting the help of their crew, their community, and neighbor Drew Kloven, owner of the downtown Lansing Great Harvest Bread Co.

They didn't know what to expect. While word of their fundraiser had spread and the holiday spirit was still strong, the weather was unpredictable and people's pocketbooks were drained from the holidays. So when six inches of heavy snow fell on the morning of their event, the O'Connors worried no one would show up.

54

But at 5:30 a.m. that morning, a stranger pulled into the little shopping strip where the bakery is located. In an act of generosity that would set the tone for the day, he plowed the area in front of Great Harvest, just in time for their 6 a.m. opening. Customers poured in and by the end of the day, the two Lansing bakeries ended up raising more than $5,500. Every penny that went into the registers that day – whether for bread, cookies, or coffee – went directly to tsunami relief efforts. "We're just a small company," says Dee, "but it sure makes us feel good knowing we can make a difference in other people's lives." The O'Connors credit their crew, who worked for free all day, and their customers for the tremendous show of support. "There was a great camaraderie and sense of significance over this event," says Bernie. "We couldn't have done it without them."

One of the best ways to find meaning is to contribute to something other than yourself. You can use work as a springboard to help the community, a charity, the environment, society, developing nations – anything that makes sense to you.

Knowing that you have helped others through your work is a tremendous source of meaning. It is direct evidence that you are making the world a better place and helping people out. It's also immensely satisfying, and a great way to get happy at work.

Go green

In the excellent documentary The Corporation, the late Ray Anderson, at the time the CEO of Interface, the world's largest carpet manufacturer, explains his rude awakening to the fact that his company could not continue to waste natural resources:

"It dawned on me that the way I'd been running Interface is the way of the plunderer. Plundering something that is not mine, something that belongs to every creature on earth.

And I said to myself, "My goodness, a day must come where this is illegal, where plundering is not allowed. I mean, it must come."

So I said to myself, "My goodness, some day people like me will end up in jail."

Interface designed and manufactured a new kind of carpet that was environmentally friendly, and while the design and production of this new product was more expensive than their regular line, it instantly became a bestseller and has made the company a fortune.

More and more companies are starting to care for the environment, and this is one area in which we can all contribute. Can you get your company to recycle paper? To use less electricity or water? To save on fuel or other resources? To start buying more environmentally friendly products? Make yourself heard, start a campaign, enlist support. Go green!

Be positive

"I have this co-worker who is almost always cheerful," says Paul, a 28-year-old schoolteacher. "It doesn't matter how busy we are, how many problems we're having, or how bad the weather is outside – he is unfailingly cheerful, relaxed, positive and optimistic, and sees the best in everything and everybody.

"He's a life-saver. There is always a positive, calm atmosphere around him, people visibly relax and become more open and constructive when they work with him, and his optimism infects others, which means that we all tend more to see solutions than problems."

"While he himself gets no more work done than anyone else, I still think he is responsible for a large part of our school's success, because his happiness at work spreads to so many other people."

Being positive is an incredibly important skill to learn, a skill that is key to both happiness and success at work. Positive people and positive workplaces choose to focus on possibilities, solutions, advantages and fun. It's not that they ignore problems, disadvantages and threats – far from it – it's just that they have found that being positive makes you both happier and more efficient. Psychological research clearly shows that they're onto something:

As a young psychology student at Pennsylvania University in the sixties, Martin Seligman was troubled. He'd designed a ground-breaking experiment, which involved giving dogs mild electric shocks that would be unpleasant but not harm them in any way. Should he go ahead and perform it? Would the potential benefits of the experiment outweigh the discomfort of the dogs? After talking it over with his advisor he went through with it and his findings shocked (no pun intended) the world of psychology.

Three dogs went through each experiment. The first dog was placed in a special cage and given electrical shocks through the floor, which stopped whenever the dog pressed a panel with its nose. It received shocks but had the power to stop them and quickly learned to do just that. The second dog got shocks whenever the first dog got them. This means that it received exactly the same amount and duration of electrical shocks as the first dog, but it had no chance to affect them. The third dog got no shocks.

Then each dog was placed in a so-called shuttlebox. Here the dog was given an electrical shock through the floor that it could easily escape by jumping over a low barrier into another part of the box. Dog number one (who'd received shocks it could turn off itself) quickly jumped over the barrier. So did dog number three that had gotten no shocks. But dog number two just lay there, feeling powerless to change its conditions. It had learned that electrical shocks were not something it could control. It had learned helplessness.

If you want to be happy at work, it's important to be positive. But how do you do that? You can't walk around all day mumbling "gotta be positive, gotta be positive" under your breath. That might make your co-workers a bit anxious …

The truth is that many workplaces have a strong focus upon the negative. Everything that goes well is ignored, while meetings focus upon problems, emails are about mistakes, phone calls mean unhappy clients, and conversations are about conflict. This constantly reinforces a sense that things are bad and there's nothing we can do to change it, and people end up like the second dog in Seligman's experiment – they give up.

Seligman's research into the field he calls positive psychology clearly shows that positive, optimistic people do much better than negative people. For example, positive people:

- Have a higher quality of life.
- Live longer.
- Are healthier.
- Do better at work.
- Experience less depression.
- Have more friends and better social lives.

And it gets better:

- Nine out of ten of the American presidential elections from 1948 to 1984 were won by the most optimistic candidate.
- Optimistic sports teams outperform pessimistic ones.

These are good solid reasons to be positive. And while Seligman's research shows that it's easy to learn negativity, pessimism and helplessness, it also shows that you can teach yourself to be positive.

In a workplace experiment, Seligman convinced an insurance company to hire a group of people who were not initially qualified to work at the company, but who all scored highly in terms of positivity and optimism. This group of employees went on to outperform all their highly skilled but less positive colleagues.

Think about it: what kind of person do you want to be at work? The positive, upbeat, happy, smiling person who works actively to make things better? Or the negative, pessimistic grouch who's already given up and accepted that things are bad and will never change?

Now, I'm not advocating constant positivity, and I think the concept of *positive thinking* is incredibly harmful. You can't always be upbeat, optimistic and happy but you can wear yourself down trying to be. Sometimes being angry, negative or pessimistic is the way to go and if it is, I say go for it. If someone treats you badly or if bad things are happening all around then being positive and cheerful might not only be hard, it might be wrong. In her fantastic book "Bright-sided – How the Tyranny of Positive Thinking is Undermining America", Barbara Ehrenreich shows how damaging it can be to force yourself and others to always be positive. In it, Ehrenreich writes:

> "In fact, there is some evidence that the ubiquitous moral injunction to think positively may place an additional burden on the already sick or otherwise aggrieved. Not only are you failing to get better but you're failing to feel good about not getting better. Similarly for the long-term unemployed, who, as I found while researching my book Bait and Switch, are informed by career coaches and self-help books that their principal battle is against their own negative, resentful, loser-like feelings. This is victim-blaming at its cruelest, and may help account for the passivity of Americans in the face of repeated economic insult.
>
> But what is truly sinister about the positivity cult is that it seems to reduce our tolerance of other people's suffering. Far from being a "culture of complaint" that upholds "victims," ours has become "less and less tolerant of people having a bad day or a bad year," according to Barbara Held, professor of psychology at Bowdoin College and a leading critic of positive psychology. If no one will listen to my problems, I won't listen to theirs: "no whining," as the popular bumper stickers and wall plaques warn. Thus the cult acquires a viral-like reproductive energy, creating an empathy deficit that pushes ever-more people into a harsh insistence on positivity in others."

So no one should be forced to be positive all the time, but you can still increase workplace happiness by increasing positivity appropriately. The following are some simple things that you can do to make yourself and the people around you more positive.

Keep a happiness-at-work log
At the end of every workday, just before you go home, take a few minutes to note down five things that made you happy at work that

day. Type the log on your computer before you shut it down, or just write it on a piece of paper. Big or small doesn't matter – note it down if it made your day a little better. Making a deadline. Talking to a nice co-worker. Meat loaf day at the cafeteria. Anything!

If you can't come up with five items for the list, just write down as many as you can. If you can't think of a single good thing, then either it's been a really bad day, or you're just not accustomed to remembering the good things that happen during the day.

Let's say you've had ten good experiences at work and one bad. If you go home thinking only of the bad one, you will remember it as a bad day. It will even feel like a bad day. Since most people have a tendency to remember negative experiences better than positive ones, it's a good idea to take extra care to remember good experiences. A happiness-at-work log is a simple, effective way to do it.

You can find a sample happiness log at this book's website: www.pinetribe.com/alexander/exercises

Have fun

A senior Southwest Airlines executive spent a day working at the ticket counter and with the ground crew in order to better understand their roles.

While she was helping direct a plane to the gate using those long orange directional devices, one of the seasoned ground crew members told her to rotate her wrists in a circular manner.

When she did this, the plane did a 360-degree turn! She began to scream, thinking she had sent a confusing signal to the pilot.

In reality, the ground crew had contacted the pilot and told them they had a "greeny" directing the plane and that they wanted to have some fun with her. The pilot enthusiastically agreed to play along[6].

Fun matters, and any job can be fun. Even in the most serious situation, fun can make work bearable.

Make room for fun at work. Give up on the idea that fun is somehow unprofessional and frivolous. Even if you're not in the mood for fun that day, let others have theirs – never ruin it for them. Just as importantly, don't force people to participate. Some are up for it that day, some aren't.

Don't worry too much about what is appropriate or proper. Fun is about being spontaneous and open. Try some things out and see what works.

Be yourself

Does your company allow you to be open and honest? Can you say what you really think? Can you show how you really feel? Can you be yourself, or do you need to hide behind a corporate, professional demeanour to be accepted?

We're much more likely to be happy at work if we can be ourselves and behave openly. Conversely, having to always hide our real thoughts and emotions will make us unhappy at work.

Say what you think

"Does it really have to be this way?"

Anna couldn't help wondering why her new boss treated her people so callously and rudely. Didn't she see that this only made them negative, cynical and demotivated?

Being the newest employee, she was in a tricky position. One that made it easy for her to see that things were not right, but difficult for her to do something about it.

Finally, after seeing her manager once again belittling a co-worker, Anna decided to do something about it. With some trepidation, she arranged a meeting with her. At the meeting she carefully explained how her boss' behaviour was affecting everyone in the department, and how she felt things should be.

To her surprise, her manager listened and gradually began trying to change her ways. With Anna's help, she has begun to praise her employees, to seek out their advice, to ask nicely rather than give orders. The manager has also discovered that this kind of behaviour is easier, more enjoyable and much more efficient than her old autocratic style.

Difficult as this may seem, the only reliable way to create openness is for each of us to say what we really think. We don't need to be rude or impolite about it, but we must express what is really going on in our minds, especially if it's something we find difficult to say. If you can't speak your mind, you're likely to be unhappy at work.

Openness also works the other way – from the company to the employees. What is your company's default approach to information?

- Almost everything is secret. We'll tell people what they need to know.
- Almost everything is open. Only a few things are secret, and only if absolutely necessary.

Most companies tend more towards secrecy, which is a mistake as far as happiness at work is concerned. Sharing important information with people makes them feel trusted and valued. If employees really know what's going on, it makes them more efficient and better able to make good decisions.

Openness also entails honesty and fairness. If a company is dishonest and unfair it's not open, and if your job doesn't allow you to be open, honest and fair, it's sure to make you unhappy.

Show what you feel

The IT support department at the medical company Leo Pharma, outside Copenhagen, Denmark, is a critical part of the organisation. If IT aren't picking up their phones, Leo's 4,000 employees have nowhere to go with their IT-related questions and problems. To ensure that the phones are always manned, a huge whiteboard with a space for each support worker shows who's at work and manning the phones at any given time.

The IT department knows that people have good days and bad days, and they're fine with that. They have a simple policy: when employees arrive in the morning, they can place a green or a red magnetic tag next to their name. Green means, "I'm having a good day," and red means, "I'm having a bad day."

When a co-worker storms in the door without saying good morning, places a red marker next to his name, and sits at his desk scowling, you don't have to wonder, "Was it something I said?"

This is a great policy that does two things:

1. It makes it visible who is having a good or a bad day, and people with red markers are given a little space and leeway. If somebody puts up a red marker every day for a week then it is clear that steps need to be taken to help that person.
2. It makes it permissible to have a bad day. We all have bad days, but if you have to hide it and pretend to be chipper, it takes longer to get out of the bad mood.

What often happens at Leo is that an employee will place a red marker in the morning, and then change it to a green one later that morning. When people are given permission to have a bad day, they recover faster and there's less chance that they will spread their bad mood to their co-workers.

It's interesting to notice the degree to which the full range of natural human emotions are not welcome in the workplace. There seems to be a widely-held belief that we're professionals at work, and professionals approach their work rationally and without emotion. Businesses would prefer us to act more like Spock, the Vulcan science officer on Star Trek, who famously said, "Emotions are alien to me. I'm a scientist."

Professor Teresa M. Amibile has been researching how working environment influences the motivation, creativity, and performance of individuals and teams. In an interview on the Harvard Business School website, she identified three main points:

1. People have incredibly rich, intense, daily inner work lives; emotions, motivations, and perceptions about their work environment permeate their daily experience at work.
2. These feelings powerfully affect people's day-to-day performance.

63

3. These feelings, which are so important for performance, are powerfully influenced by particular daily events[7].

So, we have strong emotions at work, they are affected by what goes on in the workplace, and they have a powerful impact upon our performance. Of course we do – we're human beings whether we're at work or not, and human beings have emotions.

"Emotions are alien to me. I'm an employee of Acme Inc." That is not how we work.

It's important that we show our positive emotions because that is one of the best ways to spread happiness to others, as we saw in Chapter 2. If you're really happy and don't show it, the feeling will quickly die away in you and in others.

It's also important to deal constructively with negative emotions. If something at work makes us angry, disappointed or sad and we don't act on it, three things could happen:

1. The emotion becomes stronger – Because the situation doesn't get resolved the feeling is likely to become more intense.
2. Saving it for later – Instead of dealing with your anger at the meeting that sparked it, you lash out at a co-worker later, at the server at Starbucks who forgets to put soy milk in your latte, or even at your family.
3. The ketchup effect – Feelings bottled up over a long time suddenly get released all at once and you blow up over some small matter.

All in all, it's healthier to recognise negative emotions as a sign that something is wrong and then to do something about it. I'm not saying that we should all be hyper-emotional – there are constructive ways to deal with negative emotions at work. If you're dissatisfied with something, complain constructively.

Love

Thyra Frank was head of a nursing home in Co-
penhagen for almost 25 years. She is now in her
mid-fifties, outspoken, constantly cracks jokes,
and has a loud, infectious laugh. Working in the public sector means
facing a certain set of constraints: not much money, a lot of red tape,
and very little leeway. In the face of this, she created what may be the
best functioning nursing home in Denmark.

The employees love working there, and the clients (the elderly) love
living there, because of the positive mood and the happy employees,
but also because of the weekly gala dinners with great food, wine,
live piano music, and after-dinner brandy. The residents also live on
average twice as long as in other nursing homes. The only people
who aren't crazy about her work are the authorities, because she
continues to flout the rules and do things her own way.

During her first Christmas as head, her husband persuaded her
to give the employees Christmas presents. This is not normally done
in the public sector, and the home had no budget for it. Undaunted,
Thyra went to a local supermarket and bought a cheap bottle of red
wine for each of her employees at her own expense. She also wrote
a note to each of her employees, explaining what she enjoyed about
working with that person.

It may have been a small gesture, but several of her employees
ended up crying with joy. Not so much at the cheap bottle of wine,
but at the personal, hand-written letter.

One company that understands the importance of love is Southwest
Airlines, and they even call themselves The Love Airline. Southwest
Airlines hire people first for their personality, and secondly for their
skills: "Hire for attitude, train for skill." To Southwest, a nice, sunny,
outgoing disposition matters more than degrees or experience. As a
result, Southwest is not only a happy place to work – it's also an efficient and profitable company.

Get to know the people around you at work. You don't need to make friends with everybody, but having positive relationships at work is one of the most important factors that ensure happiness at work. Positive relationships can be fostered with co-workers, employees, customers, suppliers, or even competitors.

Random acts of workplace kindness

Patricia was leaving work after a long day. She was almost the last to leave, and had to admit that she hadn't enjoyed her day much. People seemed so intent on their jobs and nobody seemed to care about the people around them.

When Patricia went into the break room to wash her coffee mug, she spotted her co-worker Lisa's unwashed mug by the sink. She quickly washed both mugs, and then, on a whim, wrote a post-it note saying, "Have a great day," drew a smiley on it and stuck it on Lisa's mug. Then she went home.

The next morning Lisa walked through the entire department with her mug in her hands and a huge smile on her face, saying "Who did this? What a great thing to do! Who was it? This totally made my morning!" Once Patricia admitted it was her, Lisa thanked her profusely. She could be found smiling broadly for a long time after. Patricia's one-minute gesture made a colleague happy at work, not just that morning but for the entire day.

It's not like there's only so much happiness at work to go around, and if others have too much, there won't be enough for you. No, the very best way to make yourself happy at work is to make others happy because:

1. Making others happy at work is a pleasure in itself.
2. Happiness is contagious, so more happy people around you means more happiness for you.
3. If you make others happy at work, there's a good chance they'll want to make you happy in return.

It's easy too:

- Bring someone a cup of coffee without them asking.
- Write a nice message on a post-it and stick it on their desk or computer.
- Offer to help with their work.
- Pass out candy.
- Leave a flower on someone's desk.
- Write someone a card.
- Take time to chat.
- Ask someone about their weekend.

There are many random acts of workplace kindness to try -- and they work wonders!

Say good morning and goodbye

David Valls Coma of Albertis Telecom in Barcelona told me this story:

"My company moved a couple of years ago. When I first arrived in the new building I met a serious security guard that looked at me like he was gruffly asking: "Who are you and where are you going?" I said good morning and entered the elevator. Next day I planned an experiment to see how a smile would change his reaction.

When I entered the building I looked at the man and wished him a good morning with a big, sincere smile on my face. I meant it, and that made him change his serious face to a grin. He wished me a good morning too.

I have been doing "the big smile experiment" ever since and it has become an anchor. Every time in, I enter the building saying "Good Morning!" with a smile, and that makes me start the day with smile in my face and in my heart.

And my relationship with the security guard is great. We chat for a moment when we run into each other, making my day, and I hope his, more enjoyable.

As the result was so good I have added this practice to my everyday life and try to give away sincere smiles to whoever I meet.

It's an unpleasant experience to come into the office happy, call out a cheerful "Good morning!" and then get nothing but reluctant, unintelligible grumblings in response.

When you arrive in the morning, make a round of your department and greet everyone there. The keys to a good greeting are to:

- Make eye contact.
- Give the person your full attention.
- Be cheerful.

When other people arrive after you, take a moment to greet them. Repeat this at the end of the day with cheerful goodbyes when you leave to go home.

It's such a simple and banal thing to do, but it makes a huge difference to relationships at the office, makes people feel more connected to each other, and establishes better communications throughout the day.

Take an interest in other people – as people

"The best boss I ever had was a woman called Linda," explains Mary, a secretary for a big Scandinavian telecommunications company. "Not only was our department consistently efficient and fun to work in, but she was rated the best manager to work for in the company year after year.

"How did she do it? Easy – she took an interest in us. She knew each of us, not only as employees but also as human beings. She not only knew about our hobbies, families, children, and lives in general – she sincerely cared about us and always had time to chat."

If all your conversations with co-workers are about goals, deadlines and tasks, it's nearly impossible to create good workplace relations. In the happiest workplaces, people care about each other not just as workers but as human beings.

Help people out

Michael, a consultant in his 40s, wanted to cheer his co-workers up a little. He came up with a great idea: one day he cleared his calendar, and announced to everyone in his department that he was available all day to help. Whatever tasks they didn't have time for, had postponed forever or found boring, he would do for them.

Michael was put to work for various co-workers throughout the day. Everyone appreciated his help, but even more importantly they had fun working together. Michael and his co-workers learned a lot about each other that day.

Workplaces in which people are constantly willing to help each other out are sure to be happier than those where people only help themselves. Helping others shows that you value them and that you want them to succeed, and it feels good because it means you can contribute actively.

I often hear people saying, "I simply don't have time to help others, I have too much work myself already." However, when everybody subscribes to this philosophy, everybody becomes less efficient, and people have even less time. If, on the other hand, you can take half an hour to help a co-worker, saving them an hour of work, and that co-worker can return the favour some day, then everybody wins. Really, we don't have time not to.

Someone has to start this trend of mutual co-operation – it might as well be you, and might as well be now!

Socialise

Kirsten Gehl, the HR manager at Accenture Denmark, and her party team, were forced to get creative. Accenture had had a rough year in 2003 and were forced to rethink their usual annual company summer party. Normally it was a huge affair held at some fancy hotel or restaurant. That was out of the question in 2003, so what would work? How could she give the people at

Accenture a much-needed positive collective experience on a much more limited budget?

First the party team decided to have the party at a smaller, cheaper and much cosier venue. Then they had the brilliant idea to get the partners to staff the bar. At first some of the partners were apprehensive, as they were known more for their dedication to work, dark suits and businesslike manner than for their ability to get down and party.

Kirsten and her party team cornered a few senior partners and garnered their support, which convinced the others to give it a try. The party became Accenture's best ever. Not only was it more fun than the traditional parties, but suddenly the partners were approachable to all employees, who could simply step up to the bar and order a gin and tonic from them. The employees loved it and, maybe most surprisingly, the partners loved it. Each of them had to be forced to leave the bar when their shifts were over!

Even after the party, the effect was felt – better relations and communication between Accenture's partners and employees.

Go bowling, go to a pub or café, have dinner at someone's house, go to the park, have an office party – anything that gives co-workers a chance to see each other outside of work and to get to know each other as people. Whatever event you choose, don't make it too traditional, fancy or expensive – make it personal and memorable instead.

Make love the foundation of your work

"The most powerful force in business isn't greed, fear, or even the raw energy of unbridled competition. The most powerful force in business is love. It's what will help your company grow and become stronger. It's what will propel your career forward. It's what will give you a sense of meaning and satisfaction in your work, which will help you do your best work."

Tim Sanders, in his excellent book Love is the Killer App

What if your work was an expression of your love for the world, for other people, for your community, and for yourself? What if you worked not only because you have to support yourself and your family, not only to advance yourself, not for the money, the title, the status symbols and the power, but because your work is a great way for you to express this love and to make a positive difference in the world?

This may seem to be a high-flying and unrealistic goal, but people who take this approach to work find that work becomes incredibly fulfilling. Everything they do becomes imbued with meaning and purpose, and their work days are spent improving people's lives – and that makes them really happy at work.

Getting results and relationships

It really is that simple to create happiness at work. Make sure that you get:

- Results
- Relationships

To get great results you must:

1. Praise
2. Grow and learn
3. Find meaning
4. Be free

To create great relationships you must:

5. Be positive
6. Be yourself
7. Love

These seven actions can be added to any activity in the workplace. Want to improve the quality of your meetings? Want to run a great project? Want to make your department a happy workplace? Ask yourself how you can help yourself and the people on the project be positive, learn, be themselves, and so on.

This is great news! This means that almost any company can become a happy place to work. Everything you need is already present or can easily be found.

Unfortunately, many people and companies don't focus their attention where it matters. They look to other, more traditional, means to create more happiness at work. Means that, unfortunately, don't work. We'll look at those in the next chapter.

3

Looking For Happiness In All The Wrong Places

~~~~~

There are three things that we traditionally strive for at work. The bad news is that they simply do not work, and pursuing them relentlessly may even be harmful to your work-happiness. They are:

1. Money, raises, bonuses and incentives.
2. Promotions, impressive titles and similar rewards.
3. Job security.

As long as we look to these three things to make us happy at work, we will get nowhere, and happiness at work will remain beyond our grasp. Let's take a closer look.

It's NOT about raises and promotions.

A high salary does not make people happy at work. Neither does a raise, a bonus, a prize, or any other kind of financial reward – except perhaps very briefly. When a person gets a raise or a bonus there is

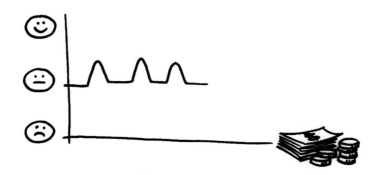

a brief spike in happiness at work, but this happiness quickly settles back to its previous level.

This does not mean that salaries don't affect our happiness at work. If you perceive your salary to be unfair, that can definitely make you unhappy. As we will see in chapter 4, being treated unfairly can make us desperately unhappy.

You should definitely fight to get the salary you deserve. If you've earned a bonus or a raise, you should get it. Also, if your salary is so low that you and your family cannot comfortably live on it, that can definitely make you unhappy.

But once your salary is fair and enough to live on, further increases in salary do not lead to an increase in happiness.

Alfie Kohn, author of the excellent and provocative book Punished by Rewards, has this to say:

> "The idea that dangling money and other goodies in front of people will "motivate" them to work harder is the conventional wisdom in our society, and particularly among compensation specialists.
>
> Rewards are not merely ineffective but actually counterproductive. Subjects offered an incentive for doing a task (or, in some of the stud-

ies, for doing it well) actually did lower quality work than subjects offered no reward at all. As University of Texas psychologist Janet Spence put it after discovering this surprising effect in an early study of her own, rewards "have effects that interfere with performance in ways that we are only beginning to understand."

Kohn's book is meticulously researched and collates results from hundreds of psychological studies. This thoroughness is essential in order to communicate Kohn's message, which is totally at odds with the way that businesses traditionally motivate employees, by throwing money and rewards at them.

A small town in the US wanted to promote reading among school children, so during the summer vacation they set up a program where children earned points for checking out books from the local library. Those points could be redeemed for free pizza at the local Domino's Pizza.

While the program ran, it was a success and the children who participated read a lot of books – and presumably got very fat on pizza. But after the program ended, these kids now read fewer books. Their own natural motivation to read books had been replaced by the external motivation of free pizza, and when the promise of pizza went away, so did the motivation.

Kohn's research found that rewarding people reduces motivation. This seems counter-intuitive at first, but Kohn's explanation is simple: every time you reward people for doing something, you motivate them externally, an act which inevitably reduces people's inner motivation. Inner motivation is the only guarantee of quality and performance in the long term.

Businesses and leaders struggle so hard to motivate their people using the promise of rewards like titles, promotions, larger offices and other corporate status symbols – but this actively lowers people's motivation.

If rewards don't work, what is the alternative? Kohn's advice is to pay people fairly and then do everything possible to not focus on rewards. Incentives, bonuses, pay-for-performance plans, and other reward systems violate that last principle by their very nature. Businesses need to stop focusing so much on offering rewards, and employees need to stop chasing them.

In summary, the truth is this:

> The salary just makes it possible for us to show up at work every day. It has no lasting effect on how happy, motivated or productive we are.

Job security

"I work in the government sector in Denmark as a *tjenestemand*, a type of civil servant, virtually immune to being fired. No matter how incompetent or obnoxious I get, I can't be fired without a huge hassle for my government department. Though the public sector is moving away from hiring people on these terms, many people still have them. No matter what they do, they won't lose their jobs. It's the ultimate job security.

It's terrible!

People end up stuck in a rut. Their world gets smaller and smaller, their focus gets more and more narrow. They also resist any and all change, no matter how small or how innocent. I hate to say this, but in many cases I really feel that firing that person would actually help them, because it would force him or her to move on."

In studies that ask people what makes them happy at work, job security often figures high on the list. It's obvious that spending each workday in fear of being fired will make you desperately unhappy. However, the kind of job security that means you're almost certain to hang on to your job no matter what happens is also bad for people's happiness at work.

Rosenbluth International, a US corporate travel agency that employed 6,000 people, faced this very dilemma. As an organisation, they had decided to put their people first and make their employees' happiness the company's top priority. But, if you've put your people first, how can you fire them?

CEO Hal Rosenbluth did not see this dilemma. To him, putting your people first entails a responsibility to fire people who don't fit in. Employees shouldn't be fired at the first sign of trouble – training, coaching, guidance, or a new position inside the company could help to motivate them. However, when these things don't work, a commitment to your employees' happiness means that you have to fire employees that don't fit in. Too much job security will actively make an organisation a less happy place to work. When people stay working in jobs where they don't fit in, you get:

- Lower performance.
- Higher workloads.
- More conflicts.
- Apathy.

Allowing an employee to stay in a job that doesn't make that employee happy is not only bad for the employee, but for everyone around that person. The unhappy employee will perform poorly, and their unhappiness at work will spread like a contagious disease.

Too little job security makes us unhappy at work because it leads to fear, avoidance of conflicts and stress. However, surprisingly, too much job security is also bad, leading to apathy, cynicism and resistance to change.

4

Warning: May Cause Severe Unhappiness

~~~~~~~~~

We've looked at what we think makes us happy at work but doesn't, and what actually makes us happy. But what makes us unhappy at work, and what can we do about it?

You can look at the things mentioned in Chapter 2. Results and relationships make people happy at work, and their absence makes people unhappy. Imagine going to work every day knowing that you will not make a difference and that you will spend the day around people who don't much care for you. Not an enticing prospect, huh?

However, aside from a lack of these positive factors, what are the major things that make us miserable on the job?

Bad bosses

"I used to be the Public Relations Coordinator and Editor for a local non-profit organisation. A couple of months before I threw in the towel my grandmother became very ill. After a phone call from a family member I was told to come to her bedside, as death was imminent.

I told my boss that I needed to leave for a family emergency and explained the situation and how close I was to my grandmother. My boss replied, "Well, she's not dead yet, so I don't have to grant your leave." And I was told to complete my workday. Suffice to say I did not finish my workday[8]."

The uncontested, number-one reason why people are unhappy at work is bad management. Nothing has more power to turn a good work situation bad than a bad boss. Sadly there are quite a lot of them around. A British study accused 1 in 4 bosses of being bad, while a Norwegian study said 1 in 5.

According to workplace researchers Sharon Jordan-Evans and Beverly Kaye, when people quit, they don't leave a company, they leave a bad boss. Surveys show that up to 75% of employees who leave their jobs do so at least in part because of their manager. In the exit interview dutifully performed by HR, employees may say that they got a higher salary or a shorter commute out of the switch, but in anonymous surveys the truth comes out: my bad boss drove me away.

The reason that having a bad manager is so bad for us is that managers have power over us. Managers can change our work situation, allocate us good or bad tasks, and, ultimately, fire us. This power imbalance is why a good relationship with your manager is so important.

What kind of manager makes people unhappy at work? A bad manager does not practice the things that make people happy at work from Chapter 2. Bad managers don't let people get results and relationships. Know any managers like that? Are you that manager, at least some of the time?

Managers face pressure to create an innovative and creative culture, one that allows employees to realise their full potential. A good manager should motivate rather than command, coach rather than control. This is possible, but only when employees are happy at work, meaning that managers must learn this new leadership style.

However, there's very little established education available on this new leadership style. So, let's cut our leaders and managers some slack. Many of them are trying hard to learn a way of working that is new to everyone.

How to deal with a bad boss

If you have a bad relationship with your boss it's vitally important that you do something about it as soon as possible. It can be tempting to wait, thinking that it might get better on its own, or that your boss might be promoted or transferred, or leave. Don't wait – do something! Here are the steps you must take.

1. Classify your boss.

Which of these three categories does your bad boss fall into?

A) Doesn't know they're bad.
B) Knows they're bad and wants to improve.
C) Doesn't want to know they're bad or doesn't want to improve.

Some managers who make their employees unhappy are simply unaware of this fact – nobody has ever told them that what they do isn't working. Some managers know that what they're doing is wrong and are trying to improve – these people need our support and good advice.

And then there's the third category: those who steadfastly refuse to acknowledge that they're bad leaders, or who revel in the fact that they make people unhappy at work. These managers are usually beyond helping and may never learn or improve. Get away from them as fast as you can.

2. Let your boss know what they could do better.

Presuming your boss is in category A or B, you must let them know what they can improve. This can be scary because of the power imbalance between managers and employees, but it needs to be done. Managers aren't mind readers, and they need honest, constructive feedback.

80

3. Assume no bad intentions.

While some of the things your boss does may make you unhappy at work, it is probably not why they do them. Assume that they mean well and are simply unaware of the effects of their actions.

4. Choose the right time to talk.

In the middle of a meeting or as a casual hallway chat are not the best ways to approach the subject. Make sure you're in a quiet undisturbed place and have time to talk about it fully.

5. Do it sooner rather than later.

It's incredibly tempting to wait and see if it gets better. Don't. Raise the issues when you notice them.

6. Explain the effects on you and the effects on your work.

Be specific and tell your manager, "When you do X it makes me do Y, which results in Z."

7. Suggest alternatives.

If you can, explain what they could do instead and why that would be better. Suggesting specific alternatives makes it easier to make positive changes.

8. Praise your manager regularly.

When your boss gets it right, remember to praise him. Many managers never receive praise because people mistakenly believe that praise should only flow from managers to employees.

You may be nervous about approaching your manager and giving him or her advice, but good managers are truly grateful for constructive, useful feedback, and will appreciate any opportunity they get to learn how to do a better job.

Difficult co-workers

Another typical cause of unhappiness at work is difficult people. Abrasive, annoying, argumentative jerks exist everywhere – including at work.

The tips in the previous section for dealing with bad bosses work equally well for dealing with these people. The main point remains the same: do something and do it now. Do not wait for the problem to go away on its own, no matter how tempting this may be.

The cult of overwork

In a feature article on workplace role models, CNN asked 12 well-known leaders, including Carlos Ghosn of Nissan, Marissa Mayer formerly of Google and famous jazz musician Wynton Marsalis, how they manage their time and stay efficient[9]. My favorite answer is as follows:

"I know that it's normal for executives to start the day extremely early, but frankly I feel I make better decisions and relate better to people when I'm well rested. So I usually get up around 8 after a good night's sleep.

I also make sure to work a standard 40-hour week and never work on the weekends. This is important to me for two reasons. First of all, I have a life outside of work. I have a family who likes to have me around, and friends and hobbies that I also want to have time for. I find that the time I spend outside of work recharges my batteries, expands my horizons, and actually makes me more efficient at work.

Secondly, if I'm always seen arriving at the office at 6 in the morning and leaving at 9 in the evening, not to mention taking calls and writing emails late at night and all weekend, it's sure to send a signal to my employees that this is what the company expects, that this is "the right way". But it isn't.

It's a simple fact that for most leaders and employees, the first 40 hours they work each week are worth much more to the company than the next 20, 30 or 40 hours. But those extra hours spent at work can harm your private life, your family and your health. Which in turn becomes damaging to the company.

Frankly, if you can't structure your time so your work fits inside a 40-hour week, you need to get better at prioritising and delegating."

Refreshing words. Guess which of the leaders said that?
NONE OF THEM.

Instead, there's a lot of, "I get up at 5 and arrive at the office at 6," "I work 16 hours a day," "I take a lot of calls on the drive in to the office," and "I usually leave the office at 7 and then work a few more hours in the evening at home."

I fully expected one of them to say, "I get up at 4 in the morning, half an hour before I go to bed, and work a 27-hour day, only stopping for a 3-minute lunch break in which two assistants stuff food down my throat like a *foie gras* goose."

This is the Cult of Overwork, the belief that the more hours you work, the better. In extreme cases this results in what the Japanese, the world champions of long work hours, call *karoshi* – death by overwork.

If you're behind at work, the solution is rarely to work more. Most of us, a few supermen and -women aside, accomplish no more in 60, 80 or 100 hours a week than we do in 40. While we may initially and for a short time get a little more work done in 80 hours than 40, there's a cost to making this the norm:

- Less creativity, because it's easier to be creative when you're relaxed.
- Worse relations with co-workers, because we're too busy to connect with people.
- Less time with friends and family.
- Less openness to new ideas – there's no time!
- Less energy and motivation.
- Lower productivity.
- Less happiness at work – because of all of the above.

As Carisa Bianchi, Chief Strategy Officer of advertising agency TBWA\Chiat\Day, puts it:

"You can always find reasons to work. There will always be one more thing to do. But when people don't take time out, they stop being productive. They stop being happy, and that affects the morale of everyone around them."

In many workplaces there's always more work, no matter how much work you finish. Everybody is always running behind, and even if you magically managed to clear your inbox, there would just be more new assignments.

You can't fix this by working harder, working longer, working more efficiently, or by prioritising your work better. You must do all of this, sure, but if there's just too much work to be done, then none of this is the solution.

"I used to work at a company with a strong "overwork" culture. After two years obsessing about getting in at 7, leaving at 7 (and then working even more from home), my wife had a baby. I took a week off, then felt justified in limiting my work to 40 hours for the next couple of months due to my lack of sleep and need to help around the house.

In that two-month period I realized I accomplished exactly as much and was exactly as busy as I was when I worked 60 hours a week. From then on, I was in at 8, out at 5, aside from the occasional large project, and I completely stopped working at home. I was never happier, more organized or more successful in that job.

All that I learned in this time enabled me to get a new job and a significantly higher salary.

Meanwhile, when I talk to employees at the old company, they're bragging about the 75-hour workweeks and discussing which anti-anxiety meds they take."

Share your comment on www.pinetribe.com/alexander/discussion

Let's once and for all drop the cult of overwork and realise that it's not the hours that count – it's the results. More hours DO NOT equate to better results.

Workplace stress and burnout

"Once upon a time there was a bear and a bee who lived in the woods and were the best of friends. All summer long the bee collected nectar from morning to night while the bear lay on his back basking in the long grass.

When winter came the bear realized he had nothing to eat and thought to himself, "I hope that busy little bee will share some of his honey with me." But the bee was nowhere to be found – he had died of a stress-induced coronary disease."

From a piece of street art by the anonymous British guerilla artist Banksy[10].

Workplace stress can be incredibly damaging to our health and quality of life. Studies show that workplace stress:

- Increases the risk of heart disease, stroke and cancer.
- Increases the risk of insomnia, depression and anxiety.
- Weakens the immune system.
- Can cause chronic muscle pain and migraines.

The costs to our workplaces are also high. According to the British Health and Safety Executive:

- Work-related stress accounts for over a third of all new incidences of ill health.
- Each case of stress-related ill health leads to an average of 30.9 working days lost.
- A total of 12.8 million working days were lost to stress, depression and anxiety in 2004/5.
- One in five people report their work as "very" or "extremely" stressful.

However, there is one fundamental misconception around stress, namely that stress comes primarily from working too much. In reality, there is little correlation between hours worked and levels of stress. It's not how much you work, it's how you feel while you work.

If you feel constantly behind and neglected, are being treated unfairly, ignored or bullied, or are going through large changes and fearing for the future, you can become stressed from working 40 hours a week. Or even 20. If this is the case, working less will not help at all. What's more, you can't fight stress – fighting stress just creates more stress.

Danish medical scientist Bo Netterstrom has been researching workplace stress for more than 30 years and clearly states:

"Happiness at work is the only lasting cure for stress."

Instead of stressing about stress, it is important to focus on what makes you calm, peaceful and happy at work, and how to get more of that. It's impossible to be both happy at work and stressed. There's an exercise to help you do just that in Chapter 5.

Celebrate the work you do

If you're feeling stressed because you're behind at work, there is one realisation that can help you:

Being stressed about being behind only makes me less efficient and is a waste of my resources.
Therefore, I will celebrate and enjoy the work I accomplish and not become stressed about the work I have yet to finish.

It's not that you shouldn't care about being behind on work – you should care. But don't become stressed about it. Instead, make sure to constantly remind yourself of the work you have accomplished, rather than beat yourself up over the work that you haven't. And always remember that working more is not the same as getting more done.

This goes double for the managers reading this. If you're always focused on the work your department has not done, you're making your people stressed – and consequently less efficient. Appreciate the work that gets done, make people happy at work, and you maximise results.

Conflicts at work

I don't know about you, but I hate conflicts at work. Spending a workday mad at a co-worker, trying to avoid that person and subconsciously finding fault with everything they say or do is not exactly my idea of a good time.

I used to be an expert at dodging conflicts on the job and I'm here to tell you that it just doesn't work! What does work is biting the bullet and doing something about it here and now. I have seen what appeared to be serious, insurmountable conflicts dissolve completely when handled constructively. But I have also seen tiny molehill-sized problems grow into mountains that threaten to topple an entire company.

You can't win a conflict at work. If you "win" a conflict you get the outcome you want regardless of what the other person wants. This can be gratifying, sure, but the problem is that the underlying issue has not been addressed. It will simply reappear later over some other topic. Much better than winning a conflict at work is resolving it.

And resolve conflict now – the price of inaction is high. Unresolved, long-running conflicts result in antagonism, a breakdown in communications, inefficient teams, stress and low productivity. In short, unresolved conflicts make people terribly unhappy at work.

With all of this in mind, here are five essential steps to help you constructively solve conflicts at work.

1. Realise that conflicts are inevitable.

Show me a workplace without conflict and I'll show you a workplace where no one gives a damn. Having a conflict at work does not mean you're a bad person – it means you're engaged enough to care. The very best and most efficient workplaces are not the ones without conflicts, but those who handle conflicts constructively.

2. Handle conflict sooner rather than later.

This is the single most important tip to successfully resolve conflicts: Do it now! It's very tempting to wait for conflicts to blow over by themselves, but they rarely do. In most cases they just get worse with time.

3. Ask!

In the early stages of a conflict the most powerful tool to resolve it is simple: instead of getting annoyed at someone, ask why they did it. Do it nicely. Say, "I was wondering why you took the last coffee yesterday without brewing some more," or "I've noticed that you often leave your cell phone unattended. Why is that?" are good examples. "Why the hell do you always have to talk so loudly on the phone?!" is less constructive.

4. Use giraffe language.

For more serious conflicts that have been going on for a while, use giraffe language. It's the best tool around for constructively conveying criticism and solving conflicts, and don't worry – no actual animal noises are involved.

Giraffe language, also known as non-violent communication, works so well because:

- It gives a difficult conversation a solid structure.
- It minimises mutual assumptions and accusations.
- It focuses on the real problems, not just the symptoms.
- It results in a plan of action, not just vague assurances to do better.

I won't give you a complete rundown of giraffe language here, but you can read all about it at this book's website.

5. Get mediation.

Some conflicts are so entrenched that they cannot be solved by the participants themselves. Outside help is needed in the form of conflict mediation, i.e., finding a third party to help find a solution. The mediator can be someone like a manager, HR employee, business coach, or co-worker.

Bureaucracy

"The place where I work is managed by good people who don't want to be bureaucratic jerks, but they can't grasp one simple concept: they are giving me money in exchange for doing something I love – they don't have to shackle me with schedules and policies to get me to produce! I will be here working my little heart out because *I want to be*.

I try to block out the memos and TPS reports and remind myself that those things aren't really changing what I get to do here, but damn, every time the red tape is thrust in my face it just deflates me and I don't even feel like trying to design or build something."

Share your comment on www.pinetribe.com/alexander/discussion

Red tape kills the soul. There you are, an employee with brilliant ideas, trying to do the best possible job, and the corporate rulebook is holding you back against common sense and everything you know to be right.

An August 2000 survey of 1,100 American employees from various organisations concluded that organisational red tape, cumbersome work rules, and tangled processes take up an extraordinary amount of time. On average, workplace bureaucracy steals 9.4 hours from the weekly schedule. For one in five people, more than 16 hours per week go down the bureaucracy drain.

Furthermore, there is a clear correlation between workplaces with more bureaucracy and workplaces people want to leave. In other words, people flee organisations burdened with red tape[11].

As CEO of Oticon, Lars Kolind went on a war against bureaucracy in his organisation. This turned Oticon around, transforming it from a marginal player to the world's leading manufacturer of hearing aids. It's a remarkable business case that is now required reading at most business schools around the world.

In his excellent book The Second Cycle: Winning the War Against Bureaucracy, Kolind writes:

"As organisations grow larger, older and more successful, they in-
troduce more management layers, more departments, more procedures, plans, budgets, reports, meetings, traditions and the like.

This leads to management developing its own agenda, increasingly detached from employees and customers. It becomes more
important to win awards than to care for customers and employees.
Management loses touch with the business, which becomes increasingly complacent and even arrogant.

This all leads to less action, slower action and no action outside
the well-known patterns."

That kind of thing makes people desperately unhappy at work, because we all want to do great work! To be held back by stupid rules
and irrational regulations makes no sense and makes your job more
complicated than it needs to be. You should read Lars' excellent book
to learn his cure for bureaucracy – and to thank him for writing a
great foreword to this book.

Bullying

"It was like a cloud of evil had descended on the factory. Everyone
was afraid of this evil.

I knew that I was being harassed and bullied, I felt like I was being forced into resigning. Every reasonable step I took to resolve my
situation was refused, or worse I was totally ignored. All the time my
treatment seemed to get harsher, I was given totally menial tasks,
which when complained about would result in me being given physically impossible tasks.

To cut a long story short I eventually suffered a breakdown. This
not only devastated me but all my family too[12]."

We human beings are highly social creatures, and feeling that we
belong is perhaps our deepest, most primal need. Bullying means
cutting a person out of the community, and singling them out for
scorn and teasing. Such treatment may seem trivial when viewed

91

from the outside, but it's not the actions of the bullies themselves that create the damage – it's the fact that the one being bullied has been excluded.

Bullying is often devastating. People break down mentally and physically, and can take years to recover. If you're being bullied, it's immensely important that you act immediately. Talk to someone. Go to your boss. Request a transfer. Quit. Whatever course of action you feel is best for you, do something.

A survey of 2,000 employees by the Chartered Institute of Personnel and Development in the UK found that 20% had experienced some form of workplace bullying or harassment in the last two years.

I cannot stress enough how dangerous this can be, and how important it is not to just wait for it to get better. If you or someone you know is being bullied at work, act now.

Negative people

Got any chronic complainers where you work? It seems like every workplace has them – the people for whom the weather is always too warm or too cold, the boss is a jerk, the food is lousy, work sucks … No matter how good things get, they still only see the bad – and they go to huge lengths to point it out to everyone around them.

I'm not saying we should outlaw complaining; it's possible to complain constructively. But we need to do something about the chronic, unconstructive complainers, because they tend to make everyone around them unhappy too. Negative people are highly contagious, and one chronic complainer can easily bring an entire department down.

There are several strategies that people typically use around complainers, none of which really work.

1. Cheering them up doesn't work.

"Oh, it can't be that bad," "Come on, cheer up," or "Time heals all wounds."

This shows the complainer that you're not taking their pain seriously. When you downplay a complainer's pain, they will often complain even harder to convince you that their problems are very serious indeed.

2. Suggesting solutions doesn't work.

"Why don't you just ...," "Have you tried ...," or "You really ought to ..."

The complainer's problems are really serious and can't be solved by a few smart-ass suggestions from you – or so they've convinced themselves. The more you try to suggest solutions, the harder they will work to convince you and themselves that these solutions could never possibly work for them.

3. Telling them to pull themselves together doesn't work.

"Quit complaining and do something about it," or one of my favourites, "You either want the problem or you want the solution."

This is telling them that their problems are trivial and they just need to pull themselves together – not a good idea.

4. Complaining about the complainers doesn't work.

"Damn, that Sally complains a lot doesn't she?"
Guess what? You just became a complainer.

5. Ignoring/avoiding them doesn't work.

This makes complainers clamour for attention, which usually makes people ignore them even more, creating a vicious circle.

6. Complaining along with them doesn't work.

"You know what, you're right – the boss is a jerk. And the weather sucks. In fact, everything sucks."

This can seem kind of cosy because it creates bonding and an us-against-the-world feeling. Ultimately, though, it's a bad idea because the more people complain, the less prone they are to do something about their problems.

I remember one of the first jobs I had where my manager was a complete dolt. My co-workers and I couldn't start a meeting, go out for a beer, or just meet in the hallway without spending 15–20 minutes complaining about him and his stupid ways. But all those man-hours spent complaining changed nothing, and none of us ever did anything about it. We all just quit the company, one by one.

So what does work? How can we stop chronic complainers from their constant grumbling? Here's a simple but very effective trick:

A friend of mine who's a dentist told me about an elderly, grouchy patient of hers who, every time he came in for an appointment, would spend most of his visit complaining about the weather, his children, his car, taxes, society, and any other topic that might come up.

Now you might think, "Hey, she's a dentist, fill his mouth with gauze and cotton and let's see him complain then!" but my friend is a naturally happy person and would instead try to cheer him up. It didn't work, it just made him complain even more.

So, I taught her this simple trick and the next time he came in for an appointment she was ready. Mr. Grouch sat in the chair and, as always, immediately started complaining.

After listening to his usual litany for a while my dentist friend said, with deep sympathy in her voice, "You know, that sounds terrible. I don't know how you deal with all of these problems."

Guess what he said?

"Weeeeell, it's not THAT bad!"

This approach works because it gives the complainer what he's really after: empathy. No cheering up, no solutions, no cheering on. Just simple, human understanding of what is, for them, a difficult situation.

There are two important things to notice here. First, don't be sarcastic when you say it. Be sincere. Secondly, you don't have to agree that these are huge problems. Even if everything the complainer says sounds trivial to you, remember that it feels like a huge problem to them or they wouldn't go on about it. What seems trivial to one person can be a huge problem for another.

So, you're not saying, "Yes, I agree that's a huge problem," and you're certainly not saying, "Oh, poor poor you," in a sarcastic voice. You're just acknowledging the fact that this is a huge problem for that person.

Does this make the complaining go away? Sometimes. But at the very least it keeps you from being part of a vicious circle of responses that just makes the complainers complain more and more and more. The circle is cut at the point where you take their distress seriously.

Boring tasks

There are no jobs out there in which every single task is fun and exciting. Any job contains boring moments, routine tasks, unpleasant assignments and contact with annoying people. Of course, if your job mostly consists of tasks you really hate to do, then maybe it's time to move on to a different job.

If your job contains occasional boring tasks, then your approach to these tasks becomes crucial. If you work with a mantra of, "This sucks, man I hate doing this, why do I always have to do it," running through your head, I can promise you that it will suck. Badly.

If you go to it with a playful attitude instead, you can make it much less unpleasant. Sometimes you can even make it fun. Here are some attitudes you can try:

- Let's do an awesome job of this.
- Let's do this 10% faster than the last time.

- Let's see if we can make it fun.
- Let's do this with full attention on the task, rather than on grumbling about it.

And there's always one more option: to not do it. Remember that people are different and the task you think is really, really boring might be a lot of fun for one of your co-workers to do. In that case it would be a shame to deprive them of the chance to do it, wouldn't it? So try to find out if somebody else would like to do the tasks you hate.

Unfairness

It turns out that a desire for fairness and equality is built into us at a biological level. Don't believe me? Try this experiment: get a bunch of Capuchin monkeys, and train them to give you a small, polished granite rock in exchange for a slice of cucumber. This is tricky in itself, but possible. Soon the monkeys learn that when they hand over the rock, they get their treat.

Then try something new: get two of these monkeys together, and give one of them a better treat. Capuchin monkeys like cucumber fine, but they like grapes even better because they're sweeter. If one capuchin sees you paying another one in grapes, it will refuse to cooperate, and will no longer hand over the rock in exchange for cucumber. "Listen, buster," it seems to say, "you're paying that guy in grapes and my work is at least as good. I want grapes too, or I'm going on strike[13]."

In another experiment using brain-scanning equipment, this time on humans, researchers found a centre in our brains that lights up whenever we believe we're being treated unfairly. It seems that fairness is not just a nice ideal to strive for – we have a biological need to be treated fairly[14].

This explains why one of the most demotivating factors in the workplace is unfairness. People react immediately to any perceived unfairness, especially when they're not happy at work. Jack Welch, ex-CEO of General Electric, tells this story from early in his career:

"My first boss, I just didn't like his methods. I thought I was doing well and I got $1,000 more – a 10 per cent raise, and I was quite pleased. I thought I was doing much more than everybody else, I thought I was performing at a different level and everyone came bouncing back with their raise and they all got $1,000. So the raise that sort of pleased me at one point now irritated the hell out of me. And so I quit. I had a baby and no money. I borrowed $1,000 bucks from my mother. I quit."

It matters less what your salary, your title, your bonus and your perks are. It matters much more whether you think they're fair. And while fairness in itself is not enough to make us happy at work, unfairness can make us desperately unhappy.

Which reminds me of the New Yorker Magazine cartoon where an employee is turned down for a raise and then promptly asks his boss "Well, if you can't give me a raise, could you at least give Peterson a pay cut?"

Fear of losing your job

Last year, Jakob, a 37-year-old IT professional, got a job he really likes in a medium-sized IT company. His boss is a great guy, his co-workers are competent and fun, and his clients are all terribly nice people.

There's only one fly in the ointment: Jakob's boss's boss (one of the VPs) is … not nice. He tends to summon all his employees to meetings and chew them over collectively and loudly for whatever problems he sees. He's abrasive and unpleasant, always complains, and never acknowledges his people for the good work they do. His emails to his underlings are a case study in rudeness. And, of course, he's known for summarily firing people who cross him in any way.

Now, while Jakob likes his job, he doesn't need it. He's independently wealthy and so skilled he can always go out and get another job, and therefore has zero fear of being fired. While other people in the company feel they must watch their tongue for fear of the consequences, he feels free to say and do exactly what he thinks is right.

And here's the thing: when Jakob stands up to this VP and tells him that he won't stand for his unpleasant approach and explains exactly why his abrasive style creates problems for the company, he listens. Nobody has ever told any VP at the company these things before, and for the first time the company has an employee that is totally unafraid of doing so.

The result: this particular VP is slowly changing his ways. And he certainly pulls none of his usual attacks on Jakob, who he knows simply won't stand for it.

The risk of being fired is the biggest axe that a company or manager holds over employees' heads. It's a mostly unstated but well-known fact of working life that if an employee gets too far out of line, they'll be fired/terminated/axed/given the chop – all terms with a dark, violent flavour ...

Of course, we've all been taught that being fired is a terrible thing that should be avoided at all costs, which is why many of us will accept bad conditions at work and go to extraordinary lengths to keep our jobs. People who live in fear of being fired tend to:

- Put up with bad treatment from management.
- Follow unethical or immoral orders.
- Stand for bullying or harassment.
- Go along to get along.
- Mask their real personalities.
- Hide their real opinions.
- Accept salaries which are too low or unfair.
- Kiss butt.
- Avoid complaining about any problems they see.

It's time we took the stigma out of being fired. If you can reduce or even rid yourself of that threat then you're granted much wider latitude at work. When you really think about it, what's so embarrassing

98

about being fired? Here are some of the most common reasons why people are fired, and why that doesn't reflect badly on the one being fired:

Personality mismatch – So you didn't fit in at that one company? There are millions of others. There will be one somewhere that is a good match for you. Besides, who says you were the problem?

Skill mismatch – So you tried out a job, and you didn't have the skills for it? Big deal. Again, there are millions of other jobs.

Refusing to go along – Good for you. If that's why you got fired, be proud for standing up for yourself.

Downsizing – Thousands of people are downsized every day.

Unreasonable firing – If you were fired for being pregnant, for telling the truth or any other unreasonable excuse, then there's certainly no reason to be ashamed.

The exceptions to this list are people who are fired for harassment, abuse, or simply not doing the job. These people need to take a closer look at themselves.

Of course, being fired can create problems, but you can deal constructively with many of them, and thus reduce or eliminate the consequences. Here are some typical problems of being fired and how to mitigate them.

Economic uncertainty

This must be the biggest problem with being fired – how will you pay your bills, your mortgage, and your kids' college savings?

There are two ways to deal with the financial problems that result from being fired. The first way is to increase your employability and make it easier to find a new job. This is a matter of keeping your personal and professional skills up to date and cultivating a good network. The second way is to keep your private expenses low, so that you're not 100% dependent upon your paycheque every month. When you're completely dependent upon bringing home a paycheque (or two) every single month you're trapped, and that makes things much worse. A bad situation is unpleasant. A bad situation you can't escape from is excruciating.

If you can reduce your personal spending to a level where you can quickly decide to not work for a while or to work for less money, you're much more free and will have a much easier time becoming happy at work. This may of course mean living in a smaller house or apartment than you would prefer, no 40-inch flatscreen TV, and no second car, but you need to ask yourself whether owning all these things is worth it. If your work makes you unhappy you're not really enjoying all the things your salary buys anyway. It makes more sense to reduce your expenses to a level that affords you more freedom at work.

Trouble explaining being fired to your next employer

If you believe that being fired is embarrassing and that it reflects badly on you, then this will come out in your CV and in your job interviews. However, if you hold your head up high and explain exactly what happened and why you're not ashamed, then this will help convey the impression that, "Yeah, I was fired, but so what?"

Some employers will understand – provided you explain it right.

Shame

Many people feel deep shame about being fired and being unemployed. Being fired from your last job is not typical polite dinner conversation with strangers. Why is being fired or unemployed so embarrassing for us? It simply doesn't need to be. Don't let others force shame upon you if you feel you have nothing to be ashamed of.

Loss of relationships

For many people, their closest relationships are with people at work – losing them can be painful. The best way to mitigate this is to make sure you have many positive relationships outside of work too. And increasing your employability helps you to quickly find a new job and establish new relationships at work.

If you reduce your fear of being fired you increase your freedom and happiness at work. At the very least you can stop feeling ashamed about something that happens to hundreds of thousands of people every year, is a perfectly natural part of working life, and which may not be your fault at all.

5

The Body At Work

~~~~~~~~~~

Physician Claus Hyldahl, an expert in work-related stress and diseases, rarely pulls any punches. In fact his style involves provoking working professionals to direct their attention to the fact that their lifestyle is bad for them. Says Hyldahl: "Many of the people who think that they're suffering from workplace stress are just out of shape. That's why they're sweating, breathing heavily, their heart is pounding and they're feeling weak. Not stress, simply bad physical shape. They don't need to reduce their workload, they need to increase their physical load."

He goes on to talk about the fact that the human body is designed to be used. "Human beings evolved from nomads and consequently evolution has optimised our bodies to a nomadic lifestyle, i.e., one that involves a lot of walking. Walking 6 miles a day is what we're built for and sitting still is bad for us. In fact, the typical, modern, sedentary way of life is as bad for your health as smoking a pack of cigarettes a day."

In many workplaces the body has been reduced to "that thing that carries the head from one meeting to the next." That's not good. Even though more and more work today is knowledge-based and goes on mainly inside people's heads, your body still matters because the body's state directly influences your mental state. If your body is tired and has no energy, you will find it very difficult to be motivated, creative and productive.

The problem is that many of the habits of the modern workplace are unhealthy. We sit still all day, eat too much, drink too much coffee, experience emotional stress and adopt unhealthy postures. The result: back problems, heart problems, weakened immune defences, diabetes, low energy, migraines, shoulder and neck pain, and much more.

It's high time that we start treating our bodies right at work.

Eat right

In a Danish study from 2005, two groups of truck drivers were given a controlled diet for two days. One group had healthy food, designed to stabilise their blood sugar levels. The other group ate junk food. Yes, the sacrifices some people make in the name of science.

The drivers were then placed in a truck simulator that tested their driving. The study found that the drivers who lived on junk food had slower reactions. When going 45 mph. on a highway, they needed 100 feet more to notice a traffic jam ahead and stop the truck than the drivers eating healthy food. Who knew that burgers could be a traffic hazard...[15]

What you eat matters a great deal for your energy, productivity and happiness at work. Controversially, the most important tip is to eat between meals. We've been told since we were children not to do it, but it's a well-known fact that when people's blood sugar drops below a certain level they get tired and grumpy. I often notice this in myself – I start getting cranky, even the smallest things annoy me, and I snap at people. An apple later, I'm fine.

Rather than eating a huge lunch meant to last you all the way until dinner, eat a smaller lunch and an afternoon snack or two. Make sure to snack on foods that take the body a long time to digest. A chocolate bar hits your body with a brief sugary energy rush and then leaves you with a lower blood sugar level, feeling more tired than before. Apples, nuts, granola bars or carrots give your body an energy boost that lasts much longer. Eat healthily and often.

Chart your energy

Here's a fun little exercise. For a week, notice how energetic you feel throughout the day and write it down hourly. You can set your watch, your phone or your calendar program to alert you once an hour.

Energy	Day 1	Day 2	Day 3	Day 4	Day 5
8 AM					
9 AM					
10 AM					
11 AM					
12 AM					
1 PM					
2 PM					
3 PM					
4 PM					
5 PM					
6 PM					

Every hour you write down how much energy you have at that particular moment on a scale from 1 to 5, where 1 = near-coma and 5 = totally energetic.

After a week, make a graph of your numbers and see if any trends emerge. Ask yourself the following questions:

- Are there some recurring peaks or slumps?
- Does your energy slump after meals? Try eating less.
- Does your energy slump between meals? A snack around that time could help.
- How does your workload and energy levels match up? Are you awake when you need to be?
- Is your energy generally low? Some exercise might be the answer.
- Is there a better way to schedule your work, depending on your energy levels?
- Are you always tired in the morning? Maybe you can start your day later. Or maybe a different breakfast is the key.

There's a 'Chart Your Energy" spreadsheet you can use for this exercise at www.pinetribe.com/alexander/exercises

Move

Your chair is your enemy! That's how the New York Times summarised the results of a study on physical activity in the workplace. It went on to say this:

> "It doesn't matter if you go running every morning, or you're a regular at the gym. If you spend most of the rest of the day sitting – in your car, your office chair, on your sofa at home – you are putting yourself at increased risk of obesity, diabetes, heart disease, a variety of cancers and an early death. In other words, irrespective of whether you exercise vigorously, sitting for long periods is bad for you."[16]

So sitting still is bad and moving around is good. As Claus Hyldahl points out, our bodies are not designed for inaction. Fortunately, there are many simple ways to add some movement to a workday:

- Stand-up meetings – Meetings also take less time that way.
- Stand up and work – Provided your desk raises to that level.

- Use a ball instead of a chair – Those big exercise balls make excellent office chairs.
- Go for a walk – Stretch your legs and get some fresh air at the same time.
- Play a game – A quick game of tag or catch is always fun.

There is also plenty of advice about the correct posture for desk-bound workers: sit up, back straight, neck straight, correct lumbar support … the list goes on. In fact, it matters less how you sit and more that you're constantly changing position. It's not that the tips are wrong, but even if your posture is picture-perfect, holding one position all day is bad for you. Change your position at the desk constantly. Put your feet up. Stand. Sit. Reverse your chair and straddle the back. Turn your chair sideways. Lie on the floor. Lean against a wall. Just move!

Sleep right

As life gets busier, both at work and outside of it, many people have cut down on their sleep time. This is not a good idea. According to the National Sleep Foundation (no I didn't know there was such a thing either), most adults need 7–9 hours of sleep a night, yet the overwhelming majority of people report that they do not get enough. When sleep deprived, people think and move more slowly, make more mistakes, and have difficulty remembering things[17].

That 7 a.m. meeting may sound like a good way to get more out of the day, but if everyone turns up tired, cranky and uncreative from lack of sleep, it may be nothing but a huge waste of time.

You can even sleep on the job. Some people find that a 15-minute powernap some time after lunch is just the ticket to staying fresh and energetic throughout the afternoon. According to the American National Institute of Mental Health, a nap enhances information processing and learning. Also, new experiments at Harvard University show that a midday snooze reverses information overload and that a 20 per cent overnight improvement in learning a motor skill is largely

105

traceable to a late stage of sleep that some early risers might be missing[18].

Make sure that you get the right amount of sleep, and the time you spend at work will be much more productive.

All the usual stuff

Yes, if you're overweight you should lose some of it. If you smoke, you should quit. If you drink too much, try moderation. If you're a coffee-holic, cut down a little. If you don't exercise, start now.

Aside from the negative health effects, each of these vices decreases your physical energy. Less energy means less motivation, drive, productivity and happiness at work. When your body is tired, your mind won't be running at full capacity either.

Me time

It's important to simply notice what's happening in your body. Take a little time out every day to reduce stress and clear your mind. Here's an exercise to help you do it.

1. Find a place where you won't be interrupted.

Somewhere with no phones, no computers, no co-workers dropping by with a quick question. Some companies are creating quiet rooms for just this purpose, but at a pinch the bathroom works just fine.

2. Close your eyes and focus on your breathing.

Just sit there for a minute or so and relax while you focus on your breathing. You don't have to breathe in any specific way, just notice it. Is it fast or slow? Is it deep or shallow? The way you breathe says a lot about your mental state. When you're angry, stressed or afraid your breathing is fast and shallow. When you're happy, relaxed and calm your breathing is deep and slow. Do this for about a minute.

3. Breathe deeply and slowly.

Just sit there with your eyes closed and take deep, slow, effortless breaths. Do this for two minutes. Your mental state affects your breath, but that link also goes the other way. Deep, slow breathing relaxes you.

4. Focus on yourself.

Ask yourself these three questions:

- A) How is my body feeling? Is there any pain? Any tense muscles? Any good feelings?
- B) What emotions am I feeling? Am I happy, angry, calm, sad, excited? All of the above?
- C) What am I thinking? What occupies my thoughts?

You don't need to do anything about any of this – just sit there for a minute and ask yourself these questions while you keep your breathing deep and slow. There are no right or wrong answers – just notice whatever comes up for you.

5. Breathe some more.

Take another minute to just sit there with your eyes closed and breathe calmly and deeply. Then, slowly open your eyes and return to work.

This simple exercise only takes five minutes out of an entire work-day, but it reduces stress, makes you more creative and gives you more energy. And, most importantly, it works as an early warning system. When work gets hectic, it's easy to miss the early signs that things are not going well. Things like tense shoulders and neck, headaches, itchiness, anger, shortness of breath, or restlessness can all be early symptoms of stress. This exercise will help you actually notice these symptoms before they become more serious and turn into migraines, depression, chronic pain, stress, or worse.

6

Why Happiness At Work Matters

~~~~~~~~~

Patricia, an outgoing, engaging, perpetually smiling woman in her early 30s with a shock of unruly, prematurely grey hair, was thrilled to get her first management job. She'd been a secretary, back-office worker and all-round administrative worker previously, but as purchasing manager for a major producer of food additives she looked forward to really streamlining their purchasing procedures.

The hiring had gone smoothly. The company needed the position filled quickly and a former colleague of Patricia who now worked there had recommended her. Everything looked great. Nice offices in a woodland setting: Check! Interesting responsibilities: Check! Nice colleagues: Check! A good salary: Absolutely!

But as Patricia started on her new job, things turned out to be less than idyllic. The mood at the company was very much one of competition rather than collaboration. Her immediate manager was rarely there, and never appreciated or even commented upon the work she or her colleagues did. In fact, nobody seemed to care what anybody else did, it was a case of "You do your job, I'll do mine."

She was doing her job, and doing it very well, but she got no recognition. Although she tried to change the mood in her department it was very difficult for the latest newcomer to change old, established ways and cultures.

As the months passed by, Patricia started to look forward to each workday less and less. It became a struggle to get out the door in the morning. She lost a lot of energy outside work. She found herself exercising less. She went out less and watched TV more.

After 7 months on the job, Patricia decided to quit. She hadn't found a new job, she simply went in and quit.

Immediately, the people close to Patricia noticed a difference: Where before she had been tired and sad, she was now happy, silly, energetic. Every day that passed after her decision to quit brought her back to herself in huge steps.

What surprised Patricia, and scared her more than a little, was that she hadn't noticed how much her job had really affected her, because that change had come very gradually over the span of months. But after her decision to quit she took the journey back to her happy self in a couple of weeks, and suddenly it became clear just how badly that unpleasant working environment had affected her, both on and off the job.

Patricia used her rediscovered energy to get a new education and is now a full-time fitness professional. Her new job makes her incredibly happy and her new workplace insists she's the "best thing that ever happened to us." Patricia has vowed never to take another job that won't make her happy.

Why does happiness at work matter? Does it matter at all, or could we all just go to work, be unhappy, collect our paycheques and be happy in our free time?

The answer is clear: not only does happiness at work matter, it is the major force that determines whether a person or a business will be successful. I know this from personal experience.

When I got my first consulting job I worked very hard. I was the picture-perfect, traditional IT consultant working many overtime hours in the name of success. I'd moved to a new city for that job, far away from my friends and family, but that was fine: I didn't really have time for anything outside of work anyway. Basically, I only focused on success at work.

After a year I suddenly realised something. I was successful, certainly, and I made good money – but I was also lonely and unhappy because all I ever did was work. I thought about that for a while, and decided to change my life, to always work in a way that would make me happy. I cut back on work and started spending time exercising and making friends in my new hometown.

Over the course of a year, my life transformed completely. Before, my evenings had consisted of the drive home from work, some fast food and lots of TV. Now I had new friends, interesting hobbies, and I was in the best shape of my life from all the exercise.

Happiness at work is not a luxury. It should not be your fifth priority after a good salary, a fancy title, a corner office and the key to the executive bathroom. Happiness is more important than anything else for determining your enjoyment of your work, your quality of life outside of work, and your success.

But we didn't used to think so.

The Protestant work ethic

Through much of our history, there has been a sense that work is hard and unpleasant and that's why we get paid to do it. This is expressed most clearly in Max Weber's biblically-based work The Protestant Work Ethic, which was used by Protestant preachers to preach that hard labour was good for people, good for Christian society, and a salve for original sin. According to Christianity, humans used to live in the Garden of Eden, where everything was perfect. But because of original sin we were ejected and, according to Genesis 3:19, this is our situation now: "By the sweat of your brow you will eat your food until you return to the ground, since from it you were taken; for dust you are and to dust you will return."

According to Hebrew belief, work is a "curse devised by God explicitly to punish the disobedience and ingratitude of Adam and Eve." The Old Testament itself supports work, not because there's any joy in it, but because it is necessary to prevent poverty and destitution.

The ancient Greek word for work is *ponos*, taken from the Latin *poena*, which means sorrow. Manual labour was for slaves, while free men were supposed to pursue warfare, large-scale commerce, and the arts, especially architecture or sculpture[19].

So, according to our cultural roots, work is a curse, a punishment for original sin, and only for slaves. In short, life is hell – or "nasty, brutish and short," as Hobbes put it – work is hell, and we must endure it because we're all sinners but don't worry, we'll get our reward once we're dead! Any questions?

It's time to put that particular view of work behind us! Richard Reeves has this to say in his excellent book Happy Mondays:

"Anybody who thinks work should be miserable simply because it is work or that there should be a *cordon sanitaire* between "work" and "life" needs to find a time machine, key in the year 1543, and go and join Calvin's crew. They'll feel more at home there. In the meantime, the rest of us will get on with enjoying our work, and our workplaces."

The scariest part of Patricia's story is how easy it is to stay in a job that makes you unhappy, partly because we're used to thinking work should be unpleasant, and partly because the negative effects sneak up on you so gradually. Think about it – did you used to be more happy, outgoing and energetic, and lost that somewhere along the way? Maybe your job is sucking the life from you. Maybe it's time to make a change and spend the majority of your working hours on something that gives you life, rather than something that slowly sucks the energy, passion and drive out of you.

Here are the major reasons to be happy at work.

Work takes up most of our time

You may spend more of your adult life on your job than on anything else, except possibly sleep. Your work will take up more of your time than your family, friends and hobbies combined. That time will be so much better spent if you're doing a job that actually makes you happy.

Work gives us most of our identity

"Work is fast replacing religion in providing meaning in people's lives. Work has become how we define ourselves, it is now answering the traditional religious questions: Who am I? How do I find meaning and purpose? Work is no longer just about economics; it's about identity."

Benjamin Hunnicutt, historian and professor at the University of Iowa at Iowa City

Just 50 years ago people had many sources of identity. Religion, class, nationality, political affiliation, family roots, and geographical and cultural origins all went into defining who we are. Today most of these, if not all, have been subsumed by work. When you meet someone at a party, what's the first question you typically ask them? Exactly: "So, what do you do?"

We are increasingly defined by our work. It's what takes up most of our time. It's where we get to use most of our skills and talents. It's where we experience our greatest triumphs and failures. It's also the basis for our standard of living. All of this means that when work is not working for us, we become very vulnerable. This is why happiness at work is crucial!

Work affects our lives in general

Patricia's story shows that being happy or unhappy at work also spills over into your private life. Some people can have a lousy day at work and then go home and be happy as if nothing has happened. However, most people can't pull this off and a bad day at work tends to affect the rest of their day.

Work affects our health

According to Professor Cary Cooper, an expert in occupational stress at the University of Manchester Institute of Science and Technology, there is an increasing body of evidence to suggest that workplace stress has a significant impact upon health.

Lancaster University and Manchester Business School performed a study in 2005 involving 250,000 employees. They found that low happiness at work is a risk factor for mental health problems, including emotional burnout, low self-esteem, anxiety and depression. The report warned that just a small drop in job satisfaction could lead to burnout of "considerable clinical importance".

A study of over 20,000 female nurses in the US over a four-year period found that unhappiness at work is just as bad for your health as smoking[20].

Not only are happy people happier, they're also healthier.

Happiness leads to success

A business coach who often coaches top executives told me that many of his sessions end with his clients realising that while they have indeed achieved all the outward signs of success, they're just not happy at work or in life. They've got the corner office, company Mercedes, million-dollar salary, and huge stock options. But ask the right questions, and it turns out that many of them are lonely and lost. Their work brings them no joy, it holds no meaning, and creates no positive, lasting relationships. It also takes up all their time and keeps

them away from their family and friends. One well-known top leader broke down crying over the realisation that most of his working life had been wasted on chasing money and power. Soon after, he quit his job and is now doing work he loves – at 1/10th his old pay.

This begs the question: What is success worth, if it doesn't make you happy? The Dalai Lama once said:

"I believe that the very purpose of our life is to seek happiness. That is clear. Whether one believes in religion or not, whether one believes in this religion or that religion, we all are seeking something better in life. So I think the very motion of our life is towards happiness ..."

He was talking about happiness in life, but the point applies equally at work. What is the point of spending most of your life at a job that doesn't make you happy? What would you feel like, lying on your deathbed, having achieved all the traditional signs of success – a huge house, flatscreen TVs in every room, lots of cars, a huge salary, a lofty title and a corner office – if your career never made you happy?

Luckily, we are seeing the emergence of a new approach to work. Work used to be something we did just to earn a living. Increasingly, the point of going to work is to be happy.

So, should we just try to be happy and forget all about success?

This is where it gets interesting: In December 2005 a group of researchers published the results of a meta-study, which combined 225 studies on happiness that had examined the lives of 225,000 people.

The researchers concluded that while success does make you happier, there is an even stronger correlation in the opposite direction, i.e., that happiness will make you successful. The study also found that happy people are more optimistic, outgoing, likeable, motivated and energetic – all essential qualities for business success[21].

This means that we don't have to sacrifice happiness for the sake of success – a depressingly common assumption these days. In fact, the opposite is true: the happier you are, the more successful you will be.

7

Happiness Is Good
For Business

~~~~~~~~~

A grande dame falls ill

Irma is the *grande dame* of Danish retail. Founded in 1870, the company is the second oldest grocery chain in the world. It's a multi-million-dollar business with 70 locations in and around Copenhagen.

However, during the 1990s the lady was ailing. The only people who still shopped there, the joke went, were little old ladies who did so mostly out of habit, because Irma was where they'd always shopped. Danes are very cost-conscious when it comes to food, and most of Irma's customers had switched to the low-cost supermarkets that had appeared all over the country. For a decade, Irma had been losing its owner a lot of money.

Switching to cheaper products to compete with the discount stores didn't work. An attempt to expand from Copenhagen to the rest of Denmark proved downright disastrous and had to be abandoned. Advertising campaigns didn't work. The owner was on the verge of either selling off Irma, closing all the stores, or converting them to their discount alternatives.

In 1999 they went with a different solution, and in one last gamble made Alfred Josefsen CEO. The softly-spoken, 42-year-old Josefsen had a plan to fix Irma's deep-set woes: "Put people first." Sure, he would improve purchasing, distribution, cost-cutting and advertising, but Alfred believed that if Irma could make its people happy at work, everything else would follow.

To achieve this, Alfred focused on some specific areas:

- Leadership training – All leaders go through leadership training focused on personal development, not on MBA skills.
- Open communications – Alfred's weekly newsletter to Irma's people is not a press release or a corporate memo. It's deeply personal and heartfelt, and has fostered trust and openness between employees and management.
- Celebrating good results – Whenever Irma needs to celebrate, all employees are invited to a huge party. Part of this involves top executives getting on stage and singing the company anthem!

Results quickly followed, and Irma became profitable less than a year after Alfred took the reins. Today Irma is the fifth-best workplace in Denmark and the best retailer to work for in Europe. Irma's employees say things like:

"Working for Irma is an honour."

"We take care of each other. If a person seems to be doing badly, it isn't just ignored."

"Management has faith in us, that we can function independently."

"Irma is the best place I have ever worked."

Additionally, in February of 2006 Irma proudly announced its best financial result ever in over 130 years of doing business. This is the result of happy people doing great work.

Alfred has described the journey in his excellent book *Kære Irma* (Dear Irma) – It's all about people, but it's unfortunately only available in Danish.

The success factor

Here's a short list of just a few of the critical success factors in business today:

- Innovation
- Customer loyalty
- Productivity
- High quality
- Great customer service
- Sales

Look familiar? Does your company face some of the same demands?

Now ask yourself where all of these things will come from. Machines? No. Improved business processes? Nah. High-priced consultants? Probably not. New IT systems? Nope. All of that can help, but is not the source of innovation, customer service, motivation or any other item on the list above.

All of these things come from people – and not just people, but happy people!

Alfred Josefsen had to improve Irma in each one of these areas. They needed innovation, they needed to cut costs, they needed to attract customers and improve service. Alfred had no doubt what his main point of attack needed to be: if he could make his people happy, all of this and more would follow.

Even if you believe that the only point of a business is to make money, you must still look after the happiness of your people, simply because studies show that happy employees will make you more money!

According to a study by the Great Place To Work Institute, which conducts annual international rankings of the world's best workplaces, happy companies are a better investment. From 1998–2012, the S&P 500 stock market index rose by 4.81%. The 100 best workplaces increased their stock prices by 14.75% in the same period – three times as much[22].

According to Denison Consulting, unhappy companies in their study had an average annual sales growth of 0.1% from 1996–2004. Happy companies grew their sales by 15.1% in the same period[23].

According to HR expert David Maister, companies that enhance employee satisfaction by 20% can improve financial performance by 42%[24].

According to Gallup, happy companies have much lower employee turnover and higher customer loyalty, sales and profit margins[25].

These and many other studies show that the main advantages a business enjoys from happiness at work are:

- Higher productivity – Happy people work faster and more efficiently.
- Higher quality – Happy employees care about quality.
- Lower absenteeism – People actually want to go to work.
- Less stress and burnout – Happy people are less prone to stress.
- Attract the best people – People want to work for you.
- Lower employee turnover – Saving huge efforts in recruiting new people.
- Higher sales – Happy people are the best salespeople.
- Higher customer satisfaction – Happy employees are the best basis for good service.
- More creativity and innovation – Happy people have more ideas.
- More adaptability – Happy people are more adaptive and open to change.
- Better stock performance – For all of the above reasons.
- A better bottom line – For all of the above reasons.

Basically, happy companies beat unhappy ones in every area, and studies confirm this again and again.

The point – in one simple graph

The jury is in and the verdict is unanimous: happy employees are guilty of improving the bottom line. Businesses don't have to choose between happiness and profits. It's not a matter of either/or. Happiness is inextricably linked with profits. Soichiro Honda, the founder of (surprise!) Honda is with me on this one:

> "Each individual should work for himself. People will not sacrifice themselves for the company. They come to work at the company to enjoy themselves."

So if you take away only one thing from this chapter, please make it this graph:

Gedankenexperiment

Let's try a *Gedankenexperiment* – a thought experiment. Imagine two different departments in the same company, department A and department B. They do pretty much the same work, work out of the same building, and are comparable in most respects.
The only difference is this:

- Department A is mostly happy. They're not deliriously happy each and every day, but the people like their jobs, like each other, and look forward to coming to work most days.

- Department B is less happy. It's not that they hate their jobs all the time, it's just that they're not crazy about them, they're not mad about each other, and though they do show up at work most of the time, it's mostly for the paycheque.

If department A (the happy one) has 10 people, how many people do you need in department B to complete the same amount of work? Think about it for a second.

Whenever I speak about happiness at work to groups of leaders, I ask them this question. The answers range from 30 (i.e., department B needs three times as many people) to 8 (i.e., department B is actually more efficient than A because they don't waste any time on being happy). Typical answers are 11, 12 or 13. As the studies quoted in this chapter show, the difference is even bigger than this, and happy employees vastly outperform unhappy ones.

Here's a bonus question for managers: what is it like to be a leader in department A compared to department B? Where would it be easier for you as a leader to:

- Motivate people.
- Initiate and implement changes.
- Create good communication.
- Create understanding of, and achieve, the company's objectives.
- Create an innovative and creative culture.

Which department would you rather lead? This question is left as an exercise to the reader.

Unhappy employees will cost you

Unhappy employees cost companies dearly. According to a University of Florida study, published in the January 2006 issue of the Journal of Applied Psychology, employees start to misbehave when they are angry at work, dislike their jobs, or believe their supervisors are unfair.

And this is not only the case for a few malcontents and complainers; even model employees turn bad and start gossiping, pilfering, backstabbing and taking long lunch breaks when they're not happy at work[26]. So not only are unhappy employees unmotivated and disengaged, but many of the people who would be exemplary employees if they were happy will actively work against the company's interest to get back at it when unhappy.

Four ways the happy companies have the unhappy beat

I want to briefly mention four specific areas in which happy companies beat unhappy ones. I've picked these because they're among the most important factors for business success today, and because many companies struggle with them.

Happy organisations are more innovative

Previously I mentioned Professor Teresa M. Amibile's research into how the work environment influences the motivation, creativity, and performance of individuals and teams. Her work shows that happy people are more creative:

"If people are in a good mood on a given day, they're more likely to have creative ideas that day, as well as the next day, even if we take into account their mood that next day.

There seems to be a cognitive process that gets set up when people are feeling good that leads to more flexible, fluent, and original thinking, and there's actually a carryover, an incubation effect, to the next day."

The Gallup Management Journal agrees, and finds that,

"59% of happy employees strongly agreed with the statement that their current job "brings out their most creative ideas," compared with only 3% of unhappy employees[27]."

So if innovation and creativity matter to your business, you need happy people.

Happy people are more motivated

"Let me be blunt. To say that the job of a leader is to motivate his followers is as ridiculous as to say the job of the Chairman of the Board of General Motors is to turn on the sun in the morning so that we may have light by which to work.

As long as we cling to the myth and magic implicit in the notion that the leader's job is to motivate the followers, that the boss's job is to motivate subordinates, that the job of development of people in our organisation is a job of motivating them, we are wasting our time."

John Paul Jones Sr.

Every leader wants motivated employees. Every employee wants to be motivated. And yet we often see managers complaining that their employees are impossible to get going, and workers complaining that their managers don't motivate them and don't know what makes them tick.

It's not the job of the manager to motivate employees. That is impossible. It's a manager's job to create a happy work environment in which employees are naturally motivated.

Think about it: how difficult must it be to motivate people who are dissatisfied, disappointed, distrustful, disengaged and unhappy at work? It's an uphill battle all the way.

An article from Harvard Business School put it like this:

"Most companies have it all wrong. They don't have to motivate their employees. They have to stop demotivating them[28]."

Happy employees need no external motivation – they motivate themselves and each other, and this internal motivation is both more efficient and more sustainable than the external motivation (like rewards) that managers of unhappy employees must resort to.

If you want true motivation in the workplace, you must create a happy workplace. It's that simple!

Happy employees deliver better customer service

A recent Harvard Business Review article entitled "Putting the Service-Profit Chain to Work" concluded that:

"When companies put employees... first, their employees are satisfied, their customers are loyal, their profits increase, and their continued success is sustained.[29]"

Happy employees make their customers happy because they:
- Are in a good mood.
- Are motivated.
- Care about customers.
- Handle difficult situations better.
- Care about quality.
- Have more energy.

Good, genuine customer service comes only from happy employees. Unhappy employees can try to fake it, but it'll be just that: fake service.

The maths is a little strange on this one: One happy employee can give ten customers a good experience. Ten unhappy employees can't give one customer a good experience – what they can do is give 100 customers a bad experience.

Happy organisations handle change better

When Poul Pabian was made CEO of a new tax office outside of Copenhagen, Denmark, created by merging five independent departments, he faced a huge challenge. The individual offices had been through too many half-baked changes already, and cynicism had set in, with employees saying, "Yeah, right, this is just one more crazy decision made over our heads. If we ignore it, it'll go away."

In such an atmosphere, it's difficult to make a merger a success, so Poul knew that he needed to do something special in order to get the employees to approach the merger with a positive attitude.

His solution was simple: he had a one-hour chat with each of his 100 new employees. This wasn't a job interview – the only purpose was to get to know his people, and to let them meet him.

He also organised for the employees themselves to paint their new offices – not to save money, but as a team-building exercise and to create ownership of the new building. People loved both ideas, and cynicism transformed to trust between management and employees. A few years later the structure of the whole Danish tax service was changed again, and Pabian's organisation now faced new mergers. How did the employees react this time? They said "A new merger? Sure, let's do it. The last time it was so easy, we're sure we can do it again."

Many companies find that change becomes more and more difficult, and that resistance to change grows inside the organisation.
Some people think that change happens only out of necessity, when the status quo becomes unbearable. These people may be surprised to learn that happy companies are much better at creating rapid, positive change than unhappy ones.

Why? Because happy companies have:

- Higher levels of trust.
- Better communication.
- Better mutual understanding.
- Greater ability to solve conflicts.
- More creativity and innovation.
- More energy and motivation.

In fact, only happy organisations can get to the point where they thrive on change, and turn one major change after another into re-sounding success stories. Unhappy organisations never reach that point and are simply left to dread the next change.

The bottom line

There is no trade-off between happiness at work and the bottom line. It's not about sacrificing one for the other. It's not a matter of either/ or – it's both or neither.

Businesses don't have to choose between profits and happiness. The real choice is this:

> Do you want your business to be rich and happy
> or poor and unhappy?

Tough choice, huh?

Let's take it a step further: Making your business happy is not just a good thing, it's the best thing you can do for any business, because it enhances everything else. Happy people learn faster, communicate better and form more efficient teams. They are more motivated, energetic and creative. Plus, happy people care about what happens to the business. Unhappy people don't give a damn – or actively wish bad things on the workplace.

This means that happiness at work makes every other activity in the workplace more efficient. Expanding the business, introducing new business processes, signing new customers, dividing or merging – whatever your business needs to do, it can do so much more efficiently when people are happy.

The future of work is happy

Our working environment is getting better. Would you want to work in today's business world or the business world of 100 years ago? 50 years ago? Even 20 years ago, sexism, discrimination and authoritarian leadership were more common than they are today. There was also less freedom, stricter codes of behaviour, less room for personal expression, and less room for professional growth and development.

Sure, some things are getting worse, particularly since the start of the financial crisis in 2008 – there is definitely more stress and anxiety in today's workplaces. But if you ask me to choose, I would absolutely prefer today's world of work over that of the 1980s, 1950s or 1920s. Even if we don't notice or think about it often, things are getting better.

If we take that thought even further, in a few years time there will mostly be happy companies. Happy companies are so much more efficient than their unhappy competitors that they will beat them in the marketplace. In fact:

> Happy companies will beat the pants off their unhappy competition!

A wave of happiness is coming to the business world. The companies who can surf that wave are bound to get more success and more happiness. Those who can't or won't will slowly sink beneath the surface. They won't be missed.

Unhappiness is just plain wrong

"Actions are right in proportion as they tend to promote happiness, wrong as they tend to produce the reverse of happiness."
John Stuart Mill

This chapter shows that businesses should embrace happiness because it's good for business. But there is one other, even more fundamental reason: making people happy is good, making them unhappy is just plain wrong!

There are workplaces out there that run their people down, make them stressed and ill, destroy their sense of self-worth, are havens for bullies, and allow all kinds of harassment. Though it is rarely intentional, these workplaces still make their people unhappy, and mentally and physically ill.

I have no idea how leaders and managers of these businesses can live with themselves. They may hide behind the old argument that companies should only care about money – or, as Milton Friedman said it, "The business of business is business." However, I hope this chapter has convinced you that this is a false argument because happy businesses make more money.

There is no longer any excuse for tolerating an unhappy work environment, when it's just as easy to create one that is inspiring, uplifting, healthy and happy – one that is good for people and good for business.

8

Who Is Responsible For Happiness At Work?

~~~~~~~~~

Helle Schier, a softly-spoken, engaging woman in her mid-20s was excited. She'd just graduated from nursing school, and had already gotten her first job as a nurse at Odense University Hospital.

But when she told a friend that she was going to work at H4, a children's ward, her friend's reaction was "Oh! I'm not sure if I should congratulate you." It turned out that H4 had quite a reputation. The nurses rarely helped each other out. The doctors disliked the nurses and the feeling was very much mutual. The nurses disliked the administrative staff, who in turn didn't feel that their work was appreciated. It was not a happy place to work.

Helle still started working there with a positive attitude, but was soon forced to agree: it was a horrible place, and working there was getting her down. She didn't like her job at all, didn't feel productive, and started to question whether being a nurse was right for her at all.

But Helle wouldn't put up with it and she wouldn't quit. She decided she would do something about it.

Whose job is it to make you happy at work? Your manager? Your co-workers? The company? Society?

Here's the truth: the ultimate responsibility for your happiness at work can only lie with you, for three simple reasons:

1. Happiness at work is an emotion. It's something totally inside of you. Only you can truly know whether you're happy at work. Only you know if things are fine, or if something needs to change.
2. Happiness at work is individual. Only you know what it takes to make you happy at work. Therefore you are responsible for making sure you have what you need to be happy.
3. Making yourself happy at work can entail some tough choices. It may mean quitting and finding a new job. It may mean unpleasant conflict, because not engaging in conflict would be even worse. It may mean battling existing corporate culture and values. You are the only one who can make the decision of whether or not to do these things. The choice and responsibility is yours.

The manager's responsibility

You might wonder what, if anything, existential philosophers like Sartre, Camus and Heidegger can teach us about modern business. The excellent book Freedom and Accountability at Work, by Peter Koestenbaum and Peter Block, shows us that their knowledge is still relevant. This quote from the book talks about motivation, but the same point applies to happiness at work:

"We currently act as if people are not inherently motivated, rather that they go to work each day and wait for someone else to light their fire. This belief is common among managers and employees alike ..."

And this belief is fundamentally wrong. We can't go to work and expect others to light our fire. It just doesn't work that way. The fire is inside you – the only person who can light it or douse it is you!

But wait just a minute! Isn't it a boss' responsibility to make their employees happy at work?! After all, if the boss is a total as... an unpleasant person, employees are sure to be unhappy at work.

To be sure, your manager has a huge influence on your happiness at work, but the ultimate responsibility is yours. Managers have three responsibilities when it comes to happiness at work. They are:

1. To make themselves happy.
2. To know and care about their people.
3. To create a mood where it's easy for people to be happy.

As a manager, your most important responsibility is to make yourself happy at work. A happy leader is a natural role model for their employees, and spreads a good mood by their very nature. An unhappy leader, no matter how well-meaning, can't reliably create that atmosphere of happiness that is necessary to allow people to do their best work.

Secondly, managers must know and care about their people. You can't lead people without a sincere interest in them and some detailed knowledge about them. How happy are they at work right now? What makes them happy or unhappy? What are their goals and dreams? Good managers know this about all their people.

Finally, good managers use this knowledge to create an environment in which it's easy to be happy. Whether or not employees take this opportunity is up to them. You can't force people to be happy, as we saw back in Chapter 1.

Obviously some managers fail completely at this, and instead manage to create atmospheres of mistrust, apathy, desperation and cutthroat competition. These managers are failing in their responsibility to happiness at work.

Other managers create a mood of happiness, positivity, openness and teamwork, and still find that some employees remain unhappy. That is not the manager's responsibility, and it never can be.

We'll look more at how managers can make their people happy at work in Chapter 10.

The company's responsibility

I once talked to a group of employees from one of Denmark's largest companies, one which is known as a very good employer. There's almost no limit to what they will do for their employees, including on-site gyms, good food, education, fresh fruit and much, much more.

But this group had a serious beef and were not satisfied. "Why," they wanted to know, "does the company Christmas present to the employees always contain red wine. Some of us prefer white you know!"

Top management's responsibility is to enable managers to create an atmosphere where it's easy to be happy at work. But as the above story shows, no matter how well you do, you can't force people to be happy – that is still their own responsibility.

The company has a responsibility to prioritise, value and reward happiness at work. It's no use for a company to say, "We want people to be happy at work," and then turn around and reward massive over-work, ruthlessness and a traditional authoritarian management style.

Here's how not to do it. Tom Markert, the global chief marketing and client service officer at ACNielsen, says this in his horrible book You Can't Win a Fight With Your Boss:

"You can forget lunch breaks. You can't make money for a company while you're eating lunch... if you don't put in the hours, someone just as smart and clever as you will. Fact of life: the strong survive.
[If you ignore this] you might just end up as roadkill – lying dead by the side of the corporate highway as others drive right past you.
I have always made a habit of walking around early and late to personally see who's pumping it out. If they are getting results and working harder than everyone else, I promote them."

Remind me never to go work for that guy!

This hardball approach is tough and testosterone-fueled – and ultimately a failure. Managers who take this attitude are actively creating an atmosphere of stress, overwork and competition. This is bad for people and bad for business.

Here's how you do it instead:

> "I began working at my organisation about a month ago and during my first "get to know my staff" meeting I informed everyone that I would prefer they work no more than 40 hours per week and that everyone take a full hour lunch.
>
> We had a big meeting last week where I asked everyone to write all their tasks on post-it notes and hang them according to a three-point scale: 1 – hate it, 2 – it's OK, 3 – love it! After rearranging tasks to be better suited for their career desires people were getting things done more quickly and leaving on time.
>
> The productivity of my team has sky-rocketed lately. People come in at 8 a.m. ready to work and excited to bring ideas to me. We all leave at 5 p.m. now as often as possible (4 out of 5 days usually) and the rest of the office seems miffed that we can "get away with it". However, with priorities realigned, people more energised about their work, and people with more time to appreciate friends and family, our work is reaching a higher caliber and output is actually increasing."
>
> Comment from Sarah Schroeder, a non-profit professional in Chicago.

Note especially that Sarah's people get more work done even though they work fewer hours.

The co-workers' responsibility

Helle got together with three other nurses from H4, all fresh out of nursing school, and they decided to do something about making their ward happy. They talked to the head nurse and got her to give them a day off in which to cook up some ideas. What they came up with was simple. First, a summer party for the staff at H4. Nothing fancy, just a garden barbecue and some silly hats. This let people met each other outside of work and established some positive personal relations.

134

Next they focused on praise. They'd heard about Kjaer Group and their Order of the Elephant. The nurses copied this, and bought a small elephant plush toy that they could pin to their uniforms. Whenever a co-worker deserves praise, that person is awarded the elephant, and they write in a journal what that person did to earn it. The journal contains entries like these:

"It makes a great difference whether Vibeke is at work or not. She makes sure everything is tidy in the office, which is a huge help for us nurses."

"It's difficult to pick one person to give the elephant to, but I'm giving it to Nina, because she is always calm, even in stressful situations, and because she is so competent."

"I think everybody at H4 deserves an elephant, but today I'm giving it to Joan because she's so great at playing with the children, big and small."

This worked really well, and soon people started noticing a difference at H4. The doctors, the nurses, the head nurse, and especially the children in the ward and their families.

Your co-workers are not responsible for your happiness at work either, and thinking "I'll be happy at work as soon as Susan stops talking loudly on the phone, John stops always criticising people and Martin stops gossiping," will get you nowhere.

You and your co-workers have a responsibility to work together to create an atmosphere in which it's easy to be happy at work. Whether people choose to be happy in that atmosphere is their own responsibility.

Your responsibility

As a result of the simple things Helle and her co-workers did, H4 is now a happy place to work, and the four nurses who got the ball rolling are teaching other departments at the hospital how to do the same. They're known inside and outside of H4 as "the happy girls".

The nurses are feeling a difference. The doctors have noticed it.

135

And the children admitted to ward and their parents have noticed a huge difference in the mood and the quality of the care given.

Here are your fundamental responsibilities around happiness at work:

1. To know what makes you happy or unhappy at work.
2. To let other people know how happy you are and what makes you happy or unhappy
3. To take action to make yourself happy at work.
4. To help create a work environment where it's easy for others to be happy at work.

As long as you sit on your butt waiting for your colleagues, manager and company to make you happy, nothing will happen. Things will start to improve only when you choose to act.

Take action and you can make a huge difference for yourself and others. The story from the H4 ward shows that it doesn't take huge resources, management backup, outside consultants or a lot of time. All it takes is a willingness to take responsibility and do something about it.

This doesn't mean that you have to go it alone. Like Helle, get other people excited about happiness at work. This makes it much easier.

But don't wait for others to do it for you. As Jerry Garcia of The Grateful Dead put it:

"Somebody has to do something, and it's just incredibly pathetic that it has to be us."

9

How To Make Yourself Happy At Work

~~~~~~~~~~

There are certainly enough things to choose from. Should you read The Seven Habits of Highly Effective People? Or the Eighth Habit? Maybe the Getting Things Done system is right for you? Is coaching what you need? Maybe some anti-stress training. Or conflict mediation. Career counselling? Or developing your communication skills, your presentation skills or your …

The truth is that your options are almost endless – and most of them are pretty good. But it's better to start somewhere else, with something even simpler. Start by making yourself happy at work.

This chapter of the book will take you through the necessary steps. The tools provided here are some that I developed for use in our workshops, and they have been used by many people in many different companies.

The exercises work really well – but only if you actually do them. If you just skim through and formulate the answers in your head, it won't make much of a difference. If you set aside some time to think and write down the answers, new thoughts and ideas may come to you.

Here are the steps you will go through:

1. How happy are you at work?
2. What makes you happy at work?
3. Visualise your goal.
4. Know your why.
5. Decide on happiness.
6. Should I stay or should I go?
7. Make a happy plan.

You can find worksheets for each of the exercises at the book's website at www.pinetribe.com/alexander/exercises

How happy are you at work?

This is where the book could have included a 200-question survey that you could fill out, add up your score and go "Yes, I'm 78.4% happy!" But seriously, you already know how you feel about your job, don't you?

When you consider everything that's good or bad about your job and the people you work with, I'm betting that you already know well enough which of these three categories you fall into:

- Argh! – I hate my job and would rather walk a mile across broken glass than ever go into work again.
- Meh![30] – My job is kinda OK. I can take it or leave it. Not too bad, not too good.
- Yay! – I love my job. It's so great, I would pay to work there. Please don't tell them I said that last part …

Take a moment to rate your current job. Where are you at, right now? In most workplace surveys, 10% say they hate their jobs and 10-20% love it. The rest, between 70 and 80% of employees, are somewhere in the middle.

If you're at Argh I can only advise you to do something about it as soon as humanly possible.

If you're already at Yay you can still decide to make your job even more enjoyable. Or, even better, choose to spread some of that work happiness to the other people at work.

Meh is dangerous because it's comfortable. It's easy to accept a nice, safe, slightly fun, slightly boring, slightly unpleasant job situation. Don't! I'm deadly serious here. Don't accept it – push for Yay. When you're at Meh, you're only a shadow of what you can be. You're using only a small fraction of yourself. You're not infecting people around you with your energy and happiness. You're not coming home every day with the knowledge that "I rocked!"

Don't settle for Meh, decide to get to Yay – then figure out what it takes to get there.

What makes you happy at work?

Think back to a situation where you were happy at work. It can be at your current job or at a previous job. It's important that you think back to a specific situation. Not just, "Man, working for Acme Inc. was great," but, say, "Man, that time at Acme two years ago where we completed the Hansen project and had a huge party – that was great." It doesn't have to be your best work experience ever – just a pretty good one.

This can be surprisingly difficult. Most people have an easier time remembering bad experiences, and thinking back to the good days takes a little work. If you can't find a single, specific nice experience at work, think back to your school days, or maybe to something you've done outside of work, say as a community volunteer, or at your children's school.

Take your time and find a specific situation where you were happy at work. Write it down. Then find two more and write them down too.

For each of the three good experiences you've remembered, write down your answers to each of the questions below. And to make it even more effective you can get together with a friend, and interview each other using the questions. The interviewer asks the questions and writes down the answers, then you switch over. You can download Exercise 1: What makes you happy at work? at the book's website at www.pinetribe.com/alexander/exercises

Ask these questions for each of your three happy work experiences and write down the answers:

1. What happened? What were the circumstances? Who was involved? What did you do?
2. How was it? What did it feel like? Why was it a good experience?
3. What did it do to the quality of your work?
4. How were your relations with co-workers, customers, suppliers and/or others at work?
5. How did it affect you outside of work?
6. Write down at least five things that made this experience possible. Which people, values, practices, tools, etc., were involved and helped make this great experience happen?
7. Write down at least five things from this experience that would you like to have more of in the future to make you happier at work.

What you've just done is an exercise based on Appreciative Inquiry, an excellent tool based on the idea that the best way to create positive change is to focus on what worked previously and what you want more of in the future, rather than on all the earlier problems you want to avoid. This exercise is great for a number of reasons:

1. You remember previous good experiences at work

It's so easy to think back to that lousy boss you had three years ago, but surprisingly difficult to think back to that great team you worked with last year. Most of us tend to take good experiences for granted and to focus more on problems, annoying people and negative situations. This exercise trains your ability to also remember good experiences – an ability that is crucial if you want to be happy at work.

2. You dig up real-life experiences

When you examine the question, "What makes me happy at work?" it's tempting to make a long list of all the traditional trappings of a good job. You know the kind of thing: a raise, a promotion, a bonus, etc. These are things we have been taught to strive for – not necessarily the things that will really make us happy.

This exercise avoids that trap because it looks back to specific situations where you were happy. These things are highly likely to work again in the future.

3. It's fun and energising

It may be difficult at first, but it's also a lot of fun to think back to the good experiences at work. Thinking back only to the bad experiences makes you feel sad and powerless. Thinking back to the good stuff gives you more energy and confidence in a positive work future for yourself.

4. You focus on what you want – not what you want to avoid

You can't choose your future work life based on what you want to avoid, because:

- We tend to get more of what we focus on. If we focus on the things we want to avoid, we unfortunately tend to get more of those.
- There are an almost infinite number of things to avoid at work. You can always add more to the list. Finding out what will make you happy is much easier and more manageable.
- Even if you managed to avoid all the things that make you unhappy at work, that still doesn't mean you'll be happy – it only means you won't be unhappy. In other words, avoiding the bad stuff can take you to Meh, but no further. To go to Yay you need to look at what makes you happy at work.

The next step is to figure out what work and life will be like once you reach your goal and become happy at work.

Visualise your goal

In this exercise you will visualise what a working day is like when you're happy at work. This exercise is important for three reasons:

1. Knowing what your goal will look, sound and feel like gives you a specific target to aim for.
2. Knowing just how great achieving your goal will feel gives you the energy to take action.
3. You focus on what you want to achieve (not on what you want to avoid), which programs your subconscious mind to achieve it.

Imagine you're at Yay – you really, really love your job. It makes you grow, it lets you learn, it gives you victories and challenges in the right measure. You wake up in the morning totally fired up about work. You don't hit that snooze button on your alarm clock five times in a row because you're just too excited about the workday ahead of you.

You have a great boss and great co-workers. Your job is interesting and fun. Every morning you come in excited; every afternoon you leave proud. You make a difference working at something meaningful. You help people around you. You are appreciated both for what you do and for who you are. Your customers love you and rave about you.

Imagine feeling this amazingly good about your work. Really put yourself there, and feel what you would feel in this situation. Now answer the following questions, as if you're already totally happy at work.

1. When you get up in the morning, how do you feel? What emotions do you have?
2. What are you thinking on your way to work?
3. As you walk in the door at work, what feeling comes over you?
4. When you greet your co-workers, what does your voice sound like? What do their voices sound like?
5. What expressions are on their faces? On your face?
6. What does your workplace sound like? Which sounds dominate?
7. You run into a problem at work. How do you react?
8. You have a disagreement with a co-worker. How do you handle it?
9. Your boss drops by to greet you as you work. What does their voice sound like? What is the expression on their face? How do you feel after your boss dropped by?
10. A co-worker asks for your help. How do you respond?
11. Your team does some amazingly great work. How do you feel? How do you celebrate it?
12. When you get home from work, how do you feel? How does your body feel?
13. What do you think about your next workday?
14. You can download a worksheet called Exercise 2: Visualise your goal on www.pinetribe.com/alexander/exercises

Know your why

The next step is to ask yourself why your life at and outside of work will be better once you're happy at work. I'm sure that if you take a good look, it's clear that being happy at work will improve your life immensely. Knowing this will give you the motivation to take action.

To find your why, ask yourself the following questions and write down your answers (you can download the worksheet Exercise 3: Know your why on www.pinetribe.com/alexander/exercises):

If I was totally happy at work, what would be different about:

1. My working day
2. My relations with co-workers
3. My relations with customers
4. My productivity
5. My motivation
6. My relations with my manager
7. My relations with my employees (if you have any)
8. My career
9. My financial situation
10. My life outside of work
11. Stress and pressure
12. My health and wellness
13. My relations with family and friends

Take a look at your answers. How is life different when you're totally happy at work? A little better? A lot better?

Knowing your goal, and why that goal is worth reaching, leaves you with one very basic choice to consider.

Decide on happiness

"Until one is committed there is hesitancy, the chance to draw back, always ineffectiveness. Concerning all acts of initiative (and creation) there is one elementary truth, the ignorance of which kills countless ideas and splendid plans:

The moment one definitely commits oneself, then Providence moves too.

All sorts of things occur to help one that would otherwise never have occurred. A whole stream of events issues from the decision, raising in one's favour all manners of unforeseen incidents and material assistance, which no man could have dreamed would have come his way."

William Murray, member of a Scottish expedition to Mount Everest

Previously I claimed that happiness at work starts with a choice: before you can make any significant progress you must decide to be happy.

Don't get me wrong – deciding to be happy won't magically make you happy. That decision is the first step.

And also remember that you're not choosing to be satisfied. You're not going for an OK work life. You're going for happiness. You're not necessarily going for irrational, exuberant, wild-eyed, magnificent levels of happiness at work, but you're definitely choosing Yay, not Meh.

That is the choice before you now. Now that you know how happy you already are at work, what it takes to make you happy, and what your life will be like when you're at Yay – will you decide to be happy at work?

Before you make that choice, remember that every decision has consequences. Choosing to be happy also means doing what it takes to get there.

If your current work situation is not good, you face the most difficult decision ...

Should I stay or should I go?

Michael felt stuck in a job he hated. Being the sales manager of an IT company may sound nice, but the reality for this father of two was stress, conflict, backstabbing, internal competition and tons of overwork.

Michael really wanted to get out but couldn't see how. His salary was great and his economic situation was just too tight. Even with his wife also working, they still only barely managed to make the payments on their house and cars. Saving up for an annual family holiday was a struggle every year and they lived in constant fear of large, unforeseen expenses.

Finally, one office power struggle became too much and Michael quit his job in disgust. He found a new job at a much nicer company, but at only half the salary and only after a few months of making no money. The family took stock of their new situation, and a depressing fact became clear: they could not afford to keep the house. After some deliberation they sold it and moved into a much smaller apartment.

A year later, Michael looked back and had this to say: "Quitting that job is the best thing I've ever done for my family and myself, and my only regret is that I didn't do it much sooner. It's true that I used to come home to a nice, big house in the suburbs. But it's also true that I usually came home too tired to play with my sons and too stressed and angry to talk to my wife.

"Now I come home at a reasonable hour, happy, relaxed and ready to enjoy family life. The kids may not love having to share a room where before they each had their own, but let me tell you this: no one in this family would trade our current situation for what we had a year ago."

Once you've decided to be happy at work, here's the most basic choice you must make: Should you try to become happy in your current job, or is it better to switch to a new job? Can you make things better where you are? Have you tried? How did it go?
There are two possible options:

1. Change is realistic. It may not be easy or fast, but things can get better at my current job.

2. Change is not realistic. The culture is too fixed or change will simply be too hard.

I'm not trying to convince you to switch jobs, and I'm not trying to convince you to stay. What I am trying to do is convince you to choose. Choose to stay where you are and make that work situation happy. Or, choose to leave and do something about it. As the philosophers say, the greatest pain is not in making one choice over another, but in not choosing at all.

Can you make changes to your current job? Remember that:

- You may not need to change the whole company. Improving the mood in your own team or department may be all that's needed.
- Often we think change is impossible, but we're simply underestimating our own ability to make a difference. Remember the story of the nurses at H4 from Chapter 8.
- There is no such thing as "A Dream Job" – any job is only as good as you make it.

Only you can know the truth of your situation, and the important thing is to give your current job a chance to make you happy, but not to break yourself trying to change the unchangeable.

Switching jobs can be a scary proposition, but for many people it's the only way they will ever be happy at work. If you decide that there is only a small chance that your current job will ever make you happy, I urge you to move on as quickly as possible. This is a decision with serious consequences, including loss of identity, prestige and financial security. Again, only you can make that choice.

If you decide to switch jobs, the other exercises in this chapter have given you a list of things to look for in your next job and a list of reasons why switching is a good thing for you. Use these results to give yourself the momentum towards a new work situation with much more happiness.

It is frighteningly easy to stay in an unhappy work situation simply for the salary and the stability. Many people do this year after year. The worst part is that the longer you put up with an unhappy job, the harder it gets to remember how much fun work can be and the harder it gets to move on and do something about it.

If you decide that you probably can't be happy in your current job, do something about it as soon as possible. In Chapter 4 there were some tips on how you can reduce the fear associated with losing your job.

Make a happy plan

It's time to make a plan. But not your typical plan – let's make a plan that actually works. We'll do this in Chapter 11.

10

What Can Managers Do?

~~~~~~~~~~~~

Complete this sentence: Our company puts the _____ first.

Hal Rosenbluth made a provocative decision: As CEO and owner of Rosenbluth International, a corporate travel agency employing 6,000 people, he decided that his company would put the employees first. Where other companies aim to satisfy customers and investors first, Rosenbluth made it their first priority to make their employees happy.

The results were spectacular: record growth, record profits and, most importantly, customers loved the exceptional service they got from Rosenbluth's happy employees. Hal Rosenbluth explained the company's approach in a book whose title elegantly sums up his philosophy: Put The Customer Second – Put Your People First And Watch 'em Kick Butt.

A company's commitment to its values is most thoroughly tested in adversity, and Rosenbluth got its share of adversity right after 9/11. Overnight, corporate travel was reduced to a fraction of its former level, and it recovered more slowly than anyone predicted.

Rosenbluth tried everything in their power to avoid layoffs. They cut expenses. Staff took pay cuts and so did managers and executives. But in the end they had to face facts: layoffs were inevitable, and they decided to fire 1,000 of their 6,000 employees. How do you handle this situation in a company that puts its people first?

In his book's most moving chapter, an epilogue written after 9/11, Hal Rosenbluth explains that though layoffs certainly don't make employees happy, not laying people off and then going bankrupt at a later date would have made even more people even more unhappy.

Hal Rosenbluth recounts how he wrote a letter to the organisation explaining the decision and the thinking behind it in detail. The result was amazing: people who'd been fired streamed into Hal's office to tell him they understood and to thank him for their time at the company.

Rosenbluth's letter also contained a pledge: that those remaining at the company would do everything they could to bring the company back on track so they could rehire those who'd been fired. Six months later, they'd hired back 500 out of the 1,000, and the company was well on its way to recovery.

This chapter is for leaders at all levels who want to spread some happiness in their team, department, division, or even across the entire business.

I hope the book so far has convinced you that happiness at work is a good thing in itself, that it will get your organisation better results, and that it will make your job as a leader easier and more fun. This chapter has a roadmap to happiness at work for your organisation:

1. Get yourself happy.
2. Make time for your people.
3. How happy are your people?
4. Visualise your happy organisation.
5. Create the business case for happiness at work.
6. Put happiness first.
7. Make a happy plan.

You can find worksheets for each of the exercises at the book's website www.pinetribe.com/alexander/exercises

Get yourself happy

A 2005 study of health care workers by researchers from the University of Minnesota found that:

Managers who were enthusiastic positively affected their employees' emotions.

Employees of unhappy managers experienced less happiness, enthusiasm and optimism, and experienced a slight increase in irritation, anger and anxiety.

A manager's leadership behaviours affect employees' emotions throughout the workday, even when the employees are not interacting with the managers[31].

When everything a manager does signals "Man, I hate my job," this attitude infects the employees. Why? Because managers have their people's attention. Whatever a manager does or says is sure to be seen and heard, and sets the tone in the organisation.

As a manager you must start by making yourself happy at work. Not at the cost of others' happiness, which is bound to fail, but in concert with others. All the tips in the previous chapters apply equally to employees and managers. Start there.

While you're working to become happy at work yourself, you can also begin to spread a good mood inside your organisation and make other people happy.

Make time for your people

Marissa Mayer, formerly Google's Vice President of Search Products & User Experience, knows how important it is for employees to have a place to go with their questions, ideas, doubts and suggestions. That's why at Google she sat in her office every day from 4 to 5:30 ready to answer any question or listen to any idea from employees.

There was a sign-up sheet on the door and couches and laptop-power outside the office for the people waiting to see her.

Many leaders have their focus exclusively on their own work, to the point where they don't have time for their employees. These leaders ignore the fact that what really matters as far as happiness at work is concerned is the day-to-day interactions they have with their people. This, more than anything, means that managers must be willing to spend time with their people.

Leaders who don't do this sacrifice their employees' efficiency to enhance their own, and they send an unmistakable message that their employees aren't valued. Here's an example:

> "My new manager seems to do his best to make his people unhappy. During our weekly department meeting, one of my co-workers asked to make an appointment with him to talk about his job. He's not happy in his job, his job may end anyway, so he wanted to discuss these issues. The manager answered: I won't have time for you the next four weeks, I've got other priorities. All of us felt punched in the stomach ..."
>
> Share your comment on www.pinetribe.com/alexander/discussion

On the other hand, managers who take time for their people make them feel appreciated, understood and motivated, creating a bond of trust. Here's how you can do it:

> "I used to work at a bank and my boss liked to celebrate when a goal was met in a very special way. He would take you to lunch or just talk to you in his office and tell you how important your achievement was.
>
> But the nice thing about the whole thing was that he explained to me just how significant my change had been to the bank operations. For example, I'm a network and security administrator. By the time we'd rebuilt the network and I'd optimized the communications with the remote offices he told me, "Thanks to you the number of credits

the bank can handle remotely has increased 200%", and that actually made me feel great. I was making a difference for this institution."

Share your comment on www.pinetribe.com/alexander/discussion

This manager took the time to personally and specifically thank employees who'd done good work, and the impact on their happiness and motivation was huge. It's impossible for managers to not take time to do this.

Also, spending time with your people is the only viable way to know how happy they are at work. Do you know how happy or unhappy your employees are?

How happy are your people?

One of Denmark's most successful small banks is from a small town called Middelfart. As a kid I lived there for a few years, and the name always caused uncontrollable giggles in my American relatives. I still have no idea why – it's a perfectly respectable name for a Danish town …

Anyway, this bank, called Middelfart Sparekasse – stop laughing, this is serious! – has chosen an inspiring mission statement:

1: We want to treat our customers in such a way that they stay with us and also recommend us to people who are not yet our customers.
2: We want to treat our employees in such a way that they look forward to coming to work every day, and are proud to tell others where they work.
3: We want to make enough money to fulfil the first two statements.

How happy is your organisation, or your corner of it? This question is typically handed over to HR, who can then distribute a job satisfaction survey that results in a lot of statistics, which can be sliced and diced in any number of ways to produce any number of results.

Which always reminds me of how Mark Twain defined three kinds of untruths – "Lies, damned lies, and statistics."

Any leader worth their salt knows how happy their people are. This is a leader's most basic responsibility, and you shouldn't need to see a bunch of pie charts – you should already know from your daily interactions with your people.

In fact, I challenge you to a simple exercise:

1. Make a list of all the people who report directly to you. If you can't make the list because you don't know all their names, that's a good place to start!
2. Next to each person, write how happy you think that person is at work: Argh, Meh or Yay.
3. Next to each number write what made you choose that score. What have you observed that person doing or saying, or not doing or saying, that led you to that particular score?

Here's an example of such a chart:

Name	Rating	Reasons for rating
Alice Smith	Yay	Always sounds positive at meetings, continually praises co-workers, greets everyone with a loud, cheerful "Good morning" every day.
Lisa Nilsson	Meh	Very quiet in meetings, never volunteers for anything, seems disengaged.
John Wallace	Argh	Looked sad at lunch last week, has called in sick often last three months.
Mia Jensen	?	Good question. Never complains but never looks particularly happy.
Mike Wagner	Yay	Always smiling, arranged that great picnic a month ago. Customers rave about him.

Download the worksheet Exercise 4: How happy are your people? At www.pinetribe.com/alexander/exercises

Can you do this exercise for all of your people or only for some? If you're not reasonably confident of all your scores, or if you're unable to rate some of your people's work-happiness, add step 4:

4. Observe your people for a few days to gather more data. Don't tell them what you're doing and don't ask them directly, just observe them. Don't be weird about it – just take a closer look at each of your people to find out how happy they are. Once you have more data, update your chart.

Then comes the last step:

5. Verify your scores. Have a fifteen-minute chat with each of your people to find out how happy they are. Ask them to rate themselves from Argh to Yay. Also, ask them what makes them happy at work and what could make them happier. And don't forget to ask them what they think of how you're doing your job.

Do this exercise now and then repeat it periodically. Every three months is great.

You may feel that you don't have the time for this exercise in your busy schedule. The truth is, you don't have time not to do it. This might cost you 15 minutes per employee every three months but it will save you enormous amounts of time in the long term. You're installing an early warning system that tells you when things are starting to go badly for any of your people, instead of only realising it when they finally blow up. You'll be helping to make them happier at work, and everyone will reap the benefits.

Don't view the time spent on this exercise as an expense – view it as an investment that's bound to repay itself many times over through increased productivity, and lower absenteeism and employee turnover.

However, there is one thing that you need to be prepared for: you may be told things about your leadership that you didn't know and won't enjoy hearing. The key here is to be open to whatever criticism or praise you receive. The definition of a great leader is not one who does everything right, but one who is always willing to learn and improve their leadership style.

Receive any input openly and constructively. Ask follow-up questions to make sure you've understood the criticism fully, and then thank the person for their honest feedback. Then you need to act on the feedback to show people that you're committed to improving as a leader and that you're truly listening to their suggestions.

Visualise your happy organisation

Knowing your goal is a great help in achieving your goal. Not just knowing it mentally and rationally, but also visually and emotionally. What does your goal look like? What will it feel like, once you achieve it? This exercise will give you a very clear picture of just that. It mirrors the exercise in the last chapter where you learned what your personal work happiness would feel like.

Imagine that you've done it. You have made your department, team or organisation totally happy. Everybody there is engaged and motivated. People love their jobs. They come in excited and leave proud. Meetings are fun and energising. Creative ideas are thrown about constantly, and many of them are carried out.

While your people are definitely having a lot of fun, they're also doing amazing work. Customers rave about the service they get from your people, and productivity and quality have never been higher.

Try to really put yourself into that future. See what you would see, and feel what you would feel if you were really there. Then, look at the following questions and write down your answers:

1. You're at home early in the morning, just before you leave for work. How do you feel about the day ahead of you?
2. You walk in the door and meet some of your people. How do they greet you? How do you greet them?

3. You're in a meeting with some of your people. What do their voices sound like? What are they saying? What does your voice sound like?
4. A new employee is starting at your organisation today. How do you receive them? What is their first impression of you? Of the workplace? Of the people working there?
5. One of your employees has done some spectacularly good work. What do you do? How does that employee receive it?
6. You need to give an employee some negative feedback. How do you do it? How does that employee receive it?
7. Your organisation has done some great work. How do you celebrate? How does it make you feel? How do your people look and sound as you celebrate you results?
8. Your organisation has failed to reach one of its goals. How do you react? How do your people react?
9. You walk through your organisation and see your people working. How do they look? What expressions are on their faces? How do they sound? What sounds dominate the workplace?
10. You come home from work. Someone asks you how your day was. What do you say? How does your voice sound as you say it? How do you feel as you say it?

A worksheet for Exercise 5: Visualize your happy organisation is available at www.pinetribe.com/alexander/exercises

There are three great things about doing this exercise:

1. Knowing what your goal will look, sound and feel like gives you a specific target to aim for.
2. Knowing just how great achieving your goal will feel gives you the energy to take action.
3. You focus on what you want to achieve (not on what you want to avoid), which programs your subconscious mind to achieve it.

The next step is to develop the arguments for doing something. Why exactly will your workplace be better when it's happy?

Create the business case for happiness at work

"People would ask me when I was talking at a business school or to an analyst group, "Which comes first, your employees, your customers or your shareholders?" And you know for a long, long time, many decades, I've been telling them that it isn't a conundrum. That if you treat your employees right, they're happy and proud and participative with respect to what they're doing. They manifest that attitude to your customers and your customers come back. And what's business all about but having your customers come back, which makes the shareholders happy?"

Herb Kelleher, ex-CEO of Southwest Airlines

Southwest Airlines has always known that great results come only from people who love their jobs, as the quote from Herb Kelleher shows, but what is the business case for happiness at work in your corner of the organisation? How will more happiness, motivation and energy improve results and the bottom line?

Take a minute to imagine, as in the previous exercise, that you've made your part of the organisation happy at work. Your people come into work totally energised, happy and motivated. They're creative, feel appreciated, take good care of the customers, and help each other out whenever they get the chance. They communicate well, praise and appreciate each other, work well as a team, and find their work meaningful.

Once your organisation, or your corner of it, is this happy, write down how this will change:

Area	Time savings	Money savings
The way you spend your time in a typical week		
Productivity and efficiency		
Customer satisfaction and loyalty		
Employee turnover and recruitment costs		
Absenteeism		
Communication		
Quality and errors		
Sales		
Change initiatives		
Creativity and innovation		
The bottom line		

In each area, try to be as specific as you can about the effects of making your organisation happy. If there are cost or time savings involved, try to estimate them. You can download the spreadsheet Exercise 6: Create the business case for happiness at work at www.pinetribe.com/alexander/exercises.

Take a look at your results and add up the savings in time and money – this will give you your business case for happiness. Now it's time to commit to happiness at work. Without this commitment, any action is likely to be hollow and ineffective.

Put happiness first

Google recognises that the key to their success is to consistently attract and hold onto the best people, and a web page listing "Top 10 Reasons to Work at Google" included these wonderful points:

159

- Life is beautiful. Being a part of something that matters and working on products in which you can believe is remarkably fulfilling.
- Appreciation is the best motivation.
- Work and play are not mutually exclusive. It is possible to code and pass the puck at the same time.
- Boldly go where no one has gone before. There are hundreds of challenges yet to solve. Your creative ideas matter here and are worth exploring. You'll have the opportunity to develop innovative new products that millions of people will find useful.

When Google announced their IPO in 2004, founders Sergey Brin and Larry Page announced that they would keep treating their employees exceptionally well. Investors who did not like this approach were kindly requested to take their money elsewhere.

In other words, Google put their people first. As a leader, are you ready to put happiness at work first? Or do you want to see your best employees defecting one by one to companies that do?

The traditional ways of motivating and engaging employees – raises, promotions, bonuses, incentives and titles – simply don't work, as we saw in Chapter 3. They can even be harmful and make people less happy and motivated.

What you need to do is both simpler and harder. Simpler, because it doesn't require you to set up complex bonus systems and results tracking. Harder, because it requires more of you as a human being. More than anything you must want positive relations with your people. You must want them to be happy.

Putting happiness first is a bold statement and might not sit well with the executives, the board, or with investors. Too bad. This is where leaders need to step up and show their conviction that a happy workforce is a great thing in itself and the best way to a better bottom line.

This is how Southwest Airlines, Rosenbluth, Irma, Google, Middelfart Sparekasse and many other great organisations get their amazing results, and they've done it by taking these three steps:

1. Put happiness at work first

Which of these two statements do you think would inspire and energise your people the most?

1. Our most important goals are to increase profits by 15%, increase stock prices by 12%, grow our market share by 8%, create 3 new divisions, and increase overseas sales by 20%. Oh, right – and to make our people happy at work.

or

2. Our most important goal is to make our people happy at work and nothing beats that priority. This is how we as a company will reach our goals together.

It's really no contest, is it? There is no way that leaders can make a company happy on their own. We need everybody on board for that, and the only way to get your employees involved is to demonstrate a heartfelt, genuine, inspiring commitment to happiness at work. That is why you must put happiness first, not at a distant 5th place to other business goals.

2. Announce these priorities to the organisation

There's no reason to keep this intention a secret – quite the contrary. People need to know that this is going on so that they can get involved. This also creates accountability so that people can hold management to it, and people can get involved in making the organisation happy.

3. Stick to these priorities

This is the difficult part – announcing that you'll put happiness first and then drifting off track when it gets too hard is worse than doing nothing. It results only in cynicism and a depressing sense that, "Yeah, management announces a lot of fancy new programs but nothing ever comes of them. We just carry on as usual until it blows over."

A clear vision of your goal and knowing exactly why this is good for you, good for your people and good for the company will help you hang onto that commitment. It's a great idea to periodically go back and review your answers to the exercises in order to boost your faith in and commitment to happiness at work.

Make a happy plan

Of course, the very best way to boost resolve and commitment to anything is to get some results from your efforts, preferably results that are fast, tangible, positive and inspiring. For that, you need a plan. But not just any plan – you need a happy plan!

11

Make A Happy Plan

~~~~~~~~

"Apathy can be overcome by enthusiasm, and enthusiasm can only
be aroused by two things: First, an ideal, with takes the imagination
by storm, and second, a definite intelligible plan for carrying that ideal
into practice."
  Arnold J. Toynbee

Happiness at work is just that: an ideal that takes the imagination by
storm. In the previous two chapters we have imagined workplaces
that are thriving, vibrant, dynamic, efficient and fun; where people
come in excited and leave proud; where they grow and learn; where
they do great work for themselves, the company and the customers;
where new ideas are constantly hatched, implemented and celebrated.
Imagine the mood. Imagine the buzz!

The other thing we need to create some sustained enthusiasm, aside
from a vision, is a plan, but let's not fall into the usual trap and:

1. Set an overly ambitious goal.
2. Make a 50-step plan complete with Gantt charts and deadlines.

3. Commit to absolutely, positively fulfil the plan no matter what.
4. Fall behind on the plan because it's difficult to take time out for your 50 action items when there's "real work" to be done.
5. Lose heart and drop the whole thing because it wasn't "important enough or you would have done it".

Does that process sound familiar? I suggest you do this instead:

1. Make a plan that's fun rather than ambitious.
2. Do one small thing every day.
3. Follow up without pressure.
4. Celebrate your results.
5. Share what you do.

In short, go for the low-hanging fruit. Get some quick, easy wins – then move on from there.

Look at the table below and fill it out. You'll notice that it only has space for five action items, and that's all you're allowed to plan. Just five actions, each of which must be:

- Fast – Something you can do now or in the next week's time.
- Easy – Something you absolutely, positively know you can do. If you're not quite sure if you can pull it off, think of something even simpler that you know you can do.
- Fun – Something you'll enjoy doing.

And, of course, it must be something that will make you and/or others a little happier at work.

5 fast, fun, easy things I will do to create more happiness at work:

1.
2.
3.
4.
5.

Then, put one more action on the plan that you feel is more challenging. Say, a difficult conversation you need to have, a decision you want to make, or even switching to a new job, if that is what you want to do.

One slightly more challenging thing I will do to create more happiness at work:

1.

The following are some tips for choosing good items for your happy plan.

Look to what makes you and others happy

We saw which actions make most people happy at work in Chapter 2. To get great results you must:

1. Praise
2. Grow and learn
3. Find meaning
4. Be free

To create great relationships you must:

1. Be positive
2. Be yourself
3. Love

Which of these do you already do in your present job? Which could you do more of? How could you do each of these more to make yourself and others a little happier?

Involve others

It's possible to go it alone, but it's much easier and much more fun to spread happiness together with others. Invite your co-workers to be a part of the project, and be sure to invite people who are sympathetic to the idea of happiness at work, particularly people who are naturally happy, fun to be around and have energy to spare.

Get together, kick some ideas around, and then try the easiest and most fun ones. This is what the nurses at the H4 children's ward did, and look how well it worked for them. We learned about their story in Chapter 8.

Go for contagious

It's even better if you can come up with an idea that is self-reproducing, i.e., one that spreads itself throughout the workplace.

You could make a list of "Reasons why our department, team or workgroup rocks". Write the first reason at the top, then pass the list to a co-worker who must do the same. When everybody has contributed, hang the paper somewhere highly visible.

Or, you could make some small "Thank you" cards to thank people for a job well done, which they can then pass on to others.

Go for something where your initial effort only needs to be very small but involves a lot of people, each of whom gets to contribute.

Give to get

It seems to be a universal principle that when there's something you want, it pays to give it to others. Would you like to receive more praise? Start praising others and they will start praising you more. Want to be surrounded by happy people? Be happy yourself. Want to be greeted with a cheerful "Good morning" every day? Start doing this yourself.

If there's anything you would like to have more of for yourself, see if you can find a way to give that to others. Give to get.

Make it fun and playful

"Fun is at the core of the way I like to do business and it has been the key to everything I've done from the outset. More than any other element, fun is the secret of Virgin's success."
Richard Branson, CEO of Virgin

The more fun and play you can inject into this process, the better. Imagine the opposite: a book that tells you that the road to happiness at work should be long, difficult and unpleasant – you'd drop the book straight away!

Try it!

You can spend days and weeks trying to come up with the perfect plan – or you can just come up with some stuff that might be fun to do, then try it. If it works, fine. If it doesn't, try something else.

Trust your instincts. If part of you really wants to try something, try it!

Make others happy

More than anything, the best way to make yourself happy at work is to make others happy. When you can spread some happiness to others, you become happy yourself, because:

- Making others happy is fun.
- They become happier and are nicer to be around.
- They might start making you happier in return.

Don't sacrifice your own happiness at work to make others happy – find ways to make other people happy that also make you happy.

Make time for happiness

If you want to get happier at work, you need to make time for it. This can be a tough proposition in today's busy work environment. You may feel that you don't have the time to spare, but the truth is exactly the opposite: you don't have the time not to do it.

Chatting with a co-worker, helping someone out, learning a new skill or contributing outside the company may take time, but it's time well spent, because when you make yourself and others happier, everyone becomes more efficient.

Say you spend 10% of your working week making yourself and others happier, and through this become 20% more efficient. Frankly, you'd be silly not to make the time.

Follow up without pressure

Once a week, say every Monday morning, take a look at your happiness plan.

When you've done one or two of the things on your list, add one or two new ones so that you always have five fast, easy, fun things and one challenging thing you want to do towards your happiness at work.

When you follow up, make sure that you:

- Don't beat yourself up over not having had enough time to do any of the things on your list. There's no rush.
- Remove any pressure to make any of the items on your plan work.

They work or they don't work – either is fine as long as you try.

Take all the pressure out of it – you can't pressure yourself into being happy.

Celebrate

When you reach your goal and become happy at work, or create a happy workplace, you need to celebrate it. There are many ways to do it, but it's vitally important to mark the occasion and celebrate your victory. You could:

- Get your department together, line everyone up and do a Mexican wave.
- Sing happy songs like "We are the champions" or "Always look on the bright side of life", the louder and more out of tune the better.
- Buy a large trophy, cup, or medal and place it in your office, the bigger and uglier the better.
- Get people together, announce the results and applaud wildly.
- Put on some music and do a victory dance, the wilder and weirder the better.
- Have a party, an additional one beside the summer and Christmas parties.

- Pass out gifts – nothing fancy or expensive, just creative and fun.
- Fill the office with balloons.
- Exchange high-fives all around.

Share what you do

If you've come up with something that works, don't keep it a secret. Share your great ideas, tips, tools and whatever else you come up with.

Share it inside your company, or even better, share it on my blog where you can tell the whole world and other readers of this book what you've done to make yourself and others happy:

www.pinetribe.com/alexander/discussion

12
Get To It

~~~~~~~~

If this book has done what I intended, you now know what happiness at work is. You have an idea what it does for people, how we achieve it, what typically makes us unhappy at work, and how we can deal with those things.

You've also read a lot of stories about happy people and happy companies. You've seen the simple, effective things they do, and I hope you have been inspired to try some of these things yourself.

But most of all, I hope you're as fired up about the idea of happiness at work as I am. Through my work I see companies where people love working, and I see people stepping up and taking charge of their work situation and making a huge difference for themselves and others. I see what it does for them – how it changes people from victims of a bad work situation to architects of a better future.

I've seen first hand the energy, creativity, buzz, passion and fun that come from being happy at work. I've seen how people grow and learn and become more themselves than ever before. I've seen people discovering new talents and skills they never knew they had. I've seen the fire in people's eyes when they are sincerely appreciated for what they do.

I know that happiness is the greatest force in business, and that being happy at work is the best way to fulfil your potential, be successful and make a positive difference. I know that the more of us get together around this vision of making work a great experience, the easier it will be to make this level of happiness the norm, rather than the exception.

I'm totally giddy about a future where almost no one will accept unhappy work, because happy, vibrant, living workplaces will have become the standard. And best of all, I know that this future is coming no matter what. The world of work is on an inevitable path towards more and more happiness. The future belongs to the happy, because the happy are just that damned good.

To make a difference, and to make ourselves and others happier at work, doesn't take a psychology degree, fancy business concepts or amazing CEO superpowers. It takes just one thing: wide-eyed enthusiasm. It won't be the MBAs, the management consultants or the business gurus who will change our workplaces for the better. It's going to be you and me and all the other people who share a complete, total, irrational belief that happiness at work is a great, great thing, and that we should do it. Now!

If you agree with me that happiness at work is a shining and inspiring goal, and want to take an active part in making it happen, there's a simple way for you to show it: Sign the manifesto! At www.pinetribe.com/alexander/manifesto , you can read the Happy At Work Manifesto, and if you agree with it, sign it to show your commitment to creating happiness at work for yourself and others.

Let's make this the springboard of a worldwide movement. Let's learn from each other, support each other, cheer each other on and celebrate our progress towards better, more efficient, more humane and happier workplaces.

Happiness at work comes from the things you and I do, here and now. There are so many things you can do – the important thing is that you do something.

Now get to it! And have great fun on the way ...

I wish you the greatest of happiness at work – and outside of it.

Alexander Kjerulf
Chief Happiness Officer

About the author

~~~~~~~~~~

ALEXANDER KJERULF is one of the world's leading experts on workplace happiness. Why? "You will spend more of your waking hours at work than anything else. If that time doesn't make you happy, it's a huge waste of life." It all makes sense when he puts it that way, doesn't it?

Perhaps by now you're thinking this is some sort of hippie doo-dah. But alas, my skeptics, this is the real deal. Alexander didn't become the leading expert on workplace happiness without a reason. He is a speaker, consultant, and author. Alexander's blog The Chief Happiness Officer is one of the world's leading blogs about careers and leadership and is read by millions of people. On the business side, he presents and conducts workshops on workplace happiness at businesses and conferences all over the world including leading organizatons like IBM, Hilton, LEGO, HP, IKEA and many others. Alex has a masters degree in computer science from The University of Southern Denmark, and is the founder of Woohoo Inc., a consultancy firm offering lectures, workshops, and leadership training with focus on happiness at work.

You can reach Alexander at pinetribe.com/alexander.

References

1 Source: money.guardian.co.uk/work/story/0,1456,1501125,00.html

2 Source: http://en.wikipedia.org/wiki/Mirror_neuron

3 Source: http://www.ncbi.nlm.nih.gov/pmc/articles/PMC3652533/

4 Source: www.wired.com/wired/archive/12.06/pixar.html

5 Source: *The Seven-Day Weekend* by Ricardo Semler. This is a great book – read it!

6 Source: Ronald Culberson's newsletter, June 2004, www.funsulting.com/h_june_2004_newsletter.html

7 Source: hbswk.hbs.edu/item/5492.html

8 Source: www.employeesurveys.com/bosses/badboss35.htm

9 Source: money.cnn.com/2006/03/02/news/newsmakers/howiwork_fortune_032006/index.htm

10 Source: www.artofthestate.co.uk/Banksy/banksy_coronary_disease.htm

11 Source: www.meaningfulworkplace.com/survey/page4.html

12 Source: www.bullyonline.org/cases/case12.htm

13 Source: news.bbc.co.uk/2/hi/science/nature/3116678.stm

14 Source: http://www.newscientist.com/article/dn16256-justice-may-be-hard-wired-into-the-human-brain.html

15 Source: http://www.tsu.dk/trafiksikkerhed_og_kost.pdf

16 Source: http://opinionator.blogs.nytimes.com/2010/02/23/stand-up-while-you-read-this/?em

17 Source: http://www.sleepfoundation.org/article/how-sleep-works/how-much-sleep-do-we-really-need

18 Source: www.nih.gov/news/pr/jul2002/nimh-02.htm

19 Source: Historical Context of the Work Ethic by Roger B. Hill, Ph.D. – www.coe.uga.edu/~rhill/workethic/hist.htm.

20 Source: news.bbc.co.uk/1/hi/health/763401.stm

21 Source: http://www.ppc.sas.upenn.edu/articlelyubomirsky.pdf

22 Source: www.greatplacetowork.com/great/graphs.php

23 Source: www.denisonconsulting.com/dc/Home/tabid/32/Default.aspx

24 Source: www.careerjournal.com/hrcenter/briefs/20010611-kennedy.html

25 Source: gmj.gallup.com/content/814/Taking-Feedback-to-the-Bottom-Line.aspx

26 Source: news.ufl.edu/2006/04/06/employee-misbehavior

27 Source: gmj.gallup.com/content/24880/Gallup-Study-Engaged-Employ-ees-Inspire-Company.aspx

28 Source: hbswk.hbs.edu/archive/5289.html

29 Source: http://hbr.org/2008/07/putting-the-service-profit-chain-to-work

30 If you're wondering what Meh means, the urban dictionary defines it as "the verbal equivalent of a shrug of the shoulders" or "an interjection used to imply indifference towards a subject". www.urbandictionary.com/define.php?term=meh

31 Source: twincities.bizjournals.com/twincities/stories/2006/02/20/daily30.html

CPSIA information can be obtained at www.ICGtesting.com
Printed in the USA
LVOW12s0335170614

390354LV00003B/11/P